Socio-Political Significance of Covenant Motif in the Old Testament

Biblical Hermeneutics Rediscovered

The Series as the name suggests will focus on Biblical Hermeneutics, i.e., literary works concerned with methods of interpreting the Old and New Testaments of Bible via different stream of topics like Literature & Poetry, Indigenous Philosophizing, Ethical response towards Ecology, Health & Healing, Science & Technology, Feminist Theology, Sociological approach towards Human Rights, Law & Politics, Arts, History of Ideas, Ancient Civilizations, Cultural Contiguity, Religious Cosmologies & Mysticism, Appraisal of various Theologians, World Peace & Harmony, Global Capitalism, Network Marketing, Cybertheology, Population & Demographics, Epigraphic Studies, Contextualized Education, and many others. We welcome a Mss. on any topic/s mentioned, whether they are original works, scholarly monographs, collections of conference papers, revised dissertations, or translations of historical documents. Through the Series we, the Publishers, are striving to put forward published works that may help Institutions, Academic Bodies, Researchers, Scholars and the World at large in furthering their respective knowledge and understanding on the concerned subject. We welcome your comments on our efforts and further suggestions on how we can enshrine new ray of analysing & explaining the written Texts through our upcoming books.

Biblical Hermeneutics Rediscovered - 31

Socio-Political Significance of Covenant Motif in the Old Testament

Reading the Theology of Prophet Jeremiah from a Tribal Perspective

Lalenkawla

Christian World Imprints

First Published in 2020 by

Christian World Imprints
Christian Publishing & Books from India
C-3, Wazirpur Industrial Area
Delhi-110052
cwidelhi2017@gmail.com
www.ChristianWorldImprints.com
Phone: +91 11 41526079

ISBN: 978-93-5148-455-4 (HB)
ISBN: 978-93-5148-456-1 (PB)

Printed in India.

The book in its original form is the thesis submitted to the Senate of Serampore College towards Master of Theology (MTh) degree and published it with permission from the Senate. The author is responsible for the contents, ideas and opinions expressed in the book. The title of the book is reframed to the present form for the purpose of publication.

Contents

Foreword

The book entitled "Socio-Political Significance of Covenant Motif in the Old Testament: Reading the Theology of Prophet Jeremiah from a Tribal Perspective" written by Lalenkawla is a timely contribution where societies in the whole world are disintegrating and moving towards individualistic ideology with capitalistic and consumeristic framework. While on the one hand, the rise and growth of globalization as a centric force has made the whole world as one small global village, on the other hand societies and the groups are more isolated in practice and greed and selfish motifs along with consumeristic value systems grow very well in our web of relationships. Human beings no longer support and help each other, rather each community try to dominate, compete and exploit for reaching apex for their supremacy.

In such a general scenario prophet Jeremiah from the Hebrew Bible has something valuable to offer. The work of Kawla reflects how Jeremiah in the ancient Israel revisits the vitality of new covenant where people need to adhere to the principles of equality, justice, peace and shalom in the midst of greed, oppression and self-centeredness. Calling the people back to the covenant and reminding them of their failure to follow old stipulations given by Yahweh, boosts the morale of Israelites by suggesting that there is still a possibility of renewing their right relationship with Yahweh by meticulously practicing the principles of covenant given to them. This covenant will be more binding and compelling which is no longer like old covenant and it will be written on their hearts rather than on the stone tablets.

By using historical critical method and particularly social scientific method Kawla skilfully exegetes Jeremianic texts on the new covenant and draws relevant implications for a contemporary Mizo society where he hails from. Not only Mizo society but all the societies in the world need to adhere to the voice of Jeremiah and return back to the cardinal principles of God's new covenant: justice, peace, righteousness, equality and shalom. Jesus Christ in the New Testament and through the new covenant has demonstrated what it means to talk and practice new covenant is our exemplary model. This book is a must read by all those who want to be part of new and alternate covenant community in the present world. I congratulate and thank Kawla for giving this valuable writing for the society at large and Mizo society in particular.

Rev. Dr. K. Jesurathnam
Friedemann Golka Professor of the Old Testament
United Theological College, Bangalore
May, 2020

Preface

The people of Israel perceived themselves as a faith community of God and alternate community in covenant with God. Throughout its history, ancient Israelite society had undergone changes and transformations. As a result of which the age-long egalitarian and communitarian values and ethics were substituted by the individualistic, exclusivist and consumerist ideologies and values, sometimes shaking the very foundation of the social order. At this juncture, the concept of covenant was in need of theological restatement and there was a shift from the old covenant to the new covenant. This new covenant was intended to provide for the necessary transition from Israel not only as a nation, but also functioned as a survival for their identity in order to create new community. Therefore, the significance of this work is that it examines the new covenant motif in the book of Jeremiah and relates it to the contemporary context of the tribals in Mizoram.

The main methodological tool employed in this research is social scientific method as well as text-centered methods such as the literary critical method. The combination of the aforementioned methods will be employed to explain the intricacies of the rhetoric of Jeremiah. The uniqueness of this investigation also lies on its perspective or reading. A Mizo tribal perspective will be utilized in order to relate the text with the Mizo context.

The findings of the study reveal that Jeremiah used several covenant traditions and formulas. It shows that the concept of covenant has been developed and changed from time to time according to the context and needs. The new covenant has distinctive characters by creating new and inclusive community, justice and righteousness. It also acts as a subversive paradigm and offers equality, solidarity, egalitarianism and communitarianism. It seeks to emancipate and liberate the community from all forms of oppression, injustice and ensures hope and comfort.

In the context of globalization with an individualistic attitude, the ethical teachings of the new covenant have great implication for the tribal community in Mizoram where there are injustices, corruptions, oppressions and discriminations. Therefore, the study proposes the Mizo traditional social ethics of *Zawlbuk* and *tlawmngaihna* as an ethical framework of the new covenant. As the new covenant brings liberation, hope, and new vision toward the community, *Zawlbuk* and *tlawmngaihna* draw the community together and transform the society through its ethical engagement and established a communitarian and harmonious society.

I am profoundly indebted to my supervisor Rev. Dr. K. Jesurathnam for his invaluable guidance, support and generous help throughout my M. Th. studies. I would also like to thank him for writing an excellent foreword for this book.

I wish also to express my heartfelt gratitude to Mr. Sudhanshu Kanda and the team of Christian World Imprints (CWI) for their efforts in publishing this book.

I am also deeply thankful to my wife Lalchhuanmawii and three children Amos, Martha and Nathan for their prayers, encouragement and support.

It is my hope and prayer that this humble book will enlighten its readers on how to effectively relate the Biblical texts according to the contextual needs of the people.

Lalenkawla

Abbreviations

AB	Anchor Bible
ABD	The Anchor Bible Dictionary
AWA	Ancient West Asia
BCE	Before Common Era
BTESSC	Board of Theological Education Senate of Serampore College
BTF	Bangalore Theological Forum
ca.	*Circa*, about, approximately
CBQ	Catholic Biblical Quarterly
Cf.,	Confer, Compare
Chap/s	Chapter/s
DTh	Doctor of Theology
e.g.,	Example
ed/s.	Editor/s or Edited by
et al.,	Others
etc.,	Lat. *et cetera*
i.e.,	(Lat. *Id est*) that is
IB	The Interpreter's Bible
IDB	The Interpreter's Dictionary of the Bible

ISPCK	Indian Society of Promoting Christian Knowledge
JSOT	Journal for the Study of Old Testament
JSS	Journal of Semitic Studies
LXX	Septuagint
MT	Masoretic Text
MTh	Master of Theology
NAC	The New American Commentary
NIB	The New Interpreter's Bible
NICOT	The New International Commentary on the Old Testament
NT	New Testament
OT	Old Testament
SEAJT	The South East Asia Journal of Theology
TDOT	Theological Dictionary of the Old Testament
Trans.	Translated by
v./vv.	Verse/verses
Viz.	(Lat. *videliet*) namely
Vol.	Volume
VT	Vetus Testamentum

Introduction

Canonical Books

1 Chr	1 Chronicles
1 Cor	1 Corinthians
1 Kings	1 Kings
1 Pet	1 Peter
1 Sam	1 Samuel
2 Chr	2 Chronicles
2 Cor	2 Corinthians
2 Kings	2 Kings
2 Sam	2 Samuel
Am	Amos
Deut	Deuteronomy
Ex	Exodus
Gen	Genesis
Heb	Hebrews
Is	Isaiah
Jer	Jeremiah
Jos	Joshua

Lam	Lamentations
Lk	Luke
Mk	Mark
Mt	Matthew
Rom	Romans

Chapter 1

Problem and Methodological Consideration

Introduction

1.1. The Problem

The people of Israel perceived themselves as a faith community of God and alternate community in covenant with God. Throughout its history, ancient Israelite society had undergone changes and transformations. As a result of which the age-long egalitarian and communitarian values and ethics were substituted by the individualistic, exclusivist and consumerist ideologies and values, sometimes shaking the very foundation of the social order. At this juncture, the concept of covenant was in need of theological restatement and there was a shift from the old covenant to the new covenant. This new covenant was intended to provide for the necessary transition from Israel not only as a nation, but also functioned as a survival for their identity in order to create new community. Therefore, the significance of this work is that it examines the new covenant motif in the book of Jeremiah and relates it to the contemporary context of the tribals in Mizoram.

The only reference to a new covenant in the Old Testament was the book of Jeremiah.[1] Jeremiah had a deep interest in the covenant between Yahweh and Israel. The word covenant (běrît) occurs some twenty-three times, most of these references to Yahweh's covenant with his people, whether the Mosaic Sinai Covenant or the new covenant,[2] but five times in connection with the covenant that Zedekiah made with the people to liberate their slaves.[3] Even where the term covenant is not used, the background to much of Jeremiah's thinking is the covenant between Yahweh and Israel perhaps chiefly the fact that Yahweh's judgment will fall on God's people for their rebellion and disobedience to God's laws. Terms like listen (obey), not to listen (disobey), law, commandments, reflect the covenant thinking.[4] The many references in Jeremiah to the Exodus show that Jeremiah was fully aware of the tradition of Israel's election at the time of the Exodus, and the idea is given great prominence.[5] Jeremiah was also aware of Yahweh's covenant with the house of David.[6] As such, in his prophecy of salvation, Jeremiah used various covenant traditions. In addition to his use of the Sinaitic Covenant of the prophecy of judgment, he employed as well the Davidic, Abrahamic and Noahic covenants. This point is very significant in an interpretation of Jeremiah. Sinaitic covenant is an obligatory covenant whereas the covenant of David, Abraham and Noah is promissory covenant.[7] Jeremiah had criticized people and leadership for breaking and abandoning

---

1 The concept of new covenant is also present in other prophetic books. Even prophets like Deutero-Isaiah, Ezekiel, Hosea and Malachi have used it without actually mentioning the term.

2 Jer 11:2,3,9,10; 14:21; 22:9; 31:31,32,33; 32:40; 33:20,21; 50:5.

3 Jer 34:8,10,13,15,18.

4 J. A. Thompson, *The Book of Jeremiah: NICOT* (Grand Rapids, Michigan: William B. Eerdmans Publishing Company, 1980), 59-60.

5 Jer 2:2-7; 7:21-22; 16:14-15; 23:7-8; 31:31-34.

6 Jer 23:5-6; cf 22:30.

7 Martin Cheng-Chang Wang, "Jeremiah and the Covenant Tradition," *SEAJT* 14/1 (1972): 9-10.

the covenant. He declares that Yahweh will inaugurate a new era with the renewed remnant community ruled under the auspices of the new covenant with a new king.[8] For Jeremiah, there is a clear contrast between the old and new covenant (Jer 31:31ff), thereby he wanted to affirm God's new creative action in the overall plan of God's redemption. As such he offers a critique on the existing social order in order to bring a radical change.[9]

Therefore, the covenant for which Jeremiah is best known is the *new covenant*.[10] Exactly what is meant by the term *new* (חָדָשׁ) has been the subject of much scholarly debate. J. P. Hyatt asserts, "The passage presents the most important single teaching of Jeremiah, where his religious thought reaches its climax and came to have great importance in the NT."[11] Further, the ethical teaching of the new covenant is marked by justice and righteousness, forgiveness, equality, committed to *torah* obedience, solidarity about the knowledge of Yahweh and so on.[12]

In the light of the above discussion, the following questions arise: What is the concept of covenant in the book of Jeremiah? Does Jeremiah develop the understanding of the new covenant in view of the impending exile experience? Will the political, socio-economic and religious contexts of the impending exile give new meaning and significance to the new covenant? In what sense is the new covenant new? Does the new covenant bring hope and liberation for the exilic community?

---

8 Kenneth Mulzac, "The Remnant and the New Covenant in the book of Jeremiah," *Andrews University Seminary Studies* 34/2 (Autumn, 1996): 242.

9 K. Jesurathnam, *Old Testament Theology: History, Issues, and Perspectives* (New Delhi: Christian World Imprints, 2016), 222.

10 Thompson, *The Book of Jeremiah: NICOT*, 579.

11 J. P. Hyatt, "The Book of Jeremiah," *IB*, vol. V, ed. G. A. Buttrick (Nashville: Abingdon Press): 786.

12 Walter Brueggemann, *A Social Reading of the Old Testament: Prophetic Approaches of Israel's Communal Life*, ed. Patrick D. Miller (Minneapolis: Fortress Press, 1994), 48.

1.2. Purpose of Research

The purpose of the research is to study the concept of the new covenant in the book of Jeremiah and thus brings out a new understanding and thereby draw its implication for the Mizo society.

1.3. Previous Research

There are several books and articles that deal with the covenant in the book of Jeremiah and it has been studied and interpreted from various perspectives. Martin Cheng-Chang Wang in his article *Jeremiah and the Covenant Tradition* reveals the intrinsic meaning of covenant with an emphasis on the theological significance of the new covenant. H. D. Potter studied *The New Covenant in Jeremiah 31:31-34* through redaction/compositional approach. He said that a few scholars have denied that this great passage originated with Jeremiah.[13] Erhard Gerstenberger, in his essay *Covenant and Commandment* explores the roots, the history and the importance of the covenant with Israel. He dealt with AWA document and compared covenant with commandment.[14] Clements in his comprehensive survey of many of the more recent studies of the prophetic writings has repeatedly demonstrated that the covenant was the *canonical principle*.[15] William J. Dumbrell in his book *Covenant and Creation: An Old Testament Covenant Theology* studied covenant from historical and form critical methods.[16] Among modern contributions the sociological and literary analysis of Brueggemann has also been very influential. However, as far as the researcher's knowledge is concerned, there are only a few or no researches been done, particularly talking about the new covenant in Jeremiah and the Church in Mizoram.

---

13 H. D. Potter, "The New Covenant in Jeremiah XXXI 31-34," *VT* 33/3 (July 1983): 347-355.

14 Erhard Gerstenberger, "Covenant and Commandment," *VT* 84/1 (March 1965): 38-51.

15 R. E. Clements, *Prophecy and Covenant* (London: SCM Press, 1965), 7.

16 William J. Dumbrell, *Covenant and Creation: An OT Covenant Theology* (Lancer: The Paternoster Press, 1984).

Thus, this research will mainly focus on the meaning and concept of the new covenant in the book of Jeremiah and its ethical implication for the community and the Church in Mizoram.

1.4. Methodology of the Present Study

The main methodological tool employed in this research is social scientific method as well as text-centered methods such as the literary critical method. The combination of the aforementioned methods will be employed to explain the intricacies of the rhetoric of Jeremiah. The uniqueness of this investigation also lies on the perspective/reading as a Mizo tribal perspective will be utilized in order to relate the text with the Mizo context.

1.4.1. Social Scientific Method

Social scientific method is to study the social structure, patterns of social life and organization of ancient Israel and all its social units so that a complete social history can be constructed and can be effective for our religious and secular life.[17] This approach is distinct from the older historical-critical approach because it does not see specific historical placement but, rather, a placement within various social voices or dynamic forces. According to Walter Brueggemann, "The use of sociological analysis in the reading of Jeremiah is complicated because of the world of the text permits the sounding of many voices."[18] It helps us to see how the covenantal perspectives of the prophetic tradition stand over against royal ideology. It yields a critique of ideology and strives towards liberation.[19] Thus, social scientific method enables us to understand the new covenant motif of hope and liberation and can be effectively utilized to connect the biblical text of Jeremiah to the contemporary context of Mizoram.

---

17 Muthunayagom, "Contemporary Approaches to Old Testament Interpretation," 182.

18 Walter Brueggemann, *A Commentary on Jeremiah: Exile and Homecoming* (Grand Rapids/Cambridge: William B. Eerdmans Publishing Company, 1998), 13.

19 Brueggemann, *A Commentary on Jeremiah: Exile and Homecoming*, 17.

1.4.2. Literary Critical Method

According to Jesurathnam, the literary method takes the biblical text and its literary character, thus appreciates the text and its mood. It gives primary importance to the text itself rather than its background.[20] Brueggemann observes that in this method, one pays attention to the power of language to propose an imaginative world and takes the world offered in the text as a possible alternative world without excessive reference to external historical factors and without excessive interest in questions of authorship.[21] Thus, the text of Jeremiah offers imaginative alternatives to established ideology that God is at work to create a new alternative community and the text continues to have power and pertinence in many subsequent contexts, including our own.[22] By applying literary critical method one can recognize the power of language that God is planning to create a new community and inclusive community. Reading the selected text from this perspective enables us to understand that the text remains a powerful tool of liberation and emancipation in our contemporary context. Therefore, the literary critical method can be instrumental in dealing the text with the ethical issues in Mizoram to create inclusive and alternate community.

1.4.3. Tribal Reading

According to K. Lallawmzuala, a Mizo perspective/a Mizo tribal reading is a new approach to the Bible. This approach can be taken as one among many new ways of contextually reading the biblical text in the present day. It is a combination of contextual, liberation and cultural-anthropological approaches of interpretation.[23] It raises questions and concerns from the Mizo tribal socio-

---

20 Kondasingu Jesurathnam, *Exploring Dalit Liberative Hermeneutics in India & The World: Based on an Ancient Hebrew Prophet, Jeremiah of Anathoth* (New Delhi: Christian World Imprints, 2015), 13.

21 Brueggemann, *A Commentary on Jeremiah: Exile and Homecoming*, 15.

22 Brueggemann, *A Commentary on Jeremiah: Exile and Homecoming*, 17.

23 K. Lallawmzuala, "Hermeneutical Issues in the Old Testament," *Mizo Journal of Theology*, 2/1 (Jan – June, 2011): 119-120. 113-125

cultural, political and economic contexts. A tribal reading should also be regarded as part of the liberation approach in so far as it is profoundly based on the common principle of the liberation hermeneutics that the interpretation of the Bible should contribute towards liberation of the poor and oppressed. However, the main concern of this hermeneutics is not only to reveal the liberative elements of the biblical texts for socio-economic liberation (unlike the Latin American liberation), but also for liberation from racial discrimination, socio-cultural assimilation and various forms of alienation.[24] Therefore, a tribal reading will uphold the significance of the tribal communitarian ways of life, cultural values and ethos, and their socio-ethical principles.

1.5. Scope and Limitation

The scope of this research is limited to the book of Jeremiah and to the selected passage, Jer 31:31-34. In addition to this, an exegetical analysis will be done in the following passages: Jer 7:1-15; 7:21-26; 11:1-13; 24:4-7; 32:36-41 to understand the whole concept of covenant in Jeremiah. Through the study of these texts the researcher will bring the ethical implication to the Church in Mizoram.

1.6. Chapters' Outline

The present chapter, i.e., first chapter introduces the research and sets the stage for the entire research problem. Introductory issues like nature of the problem, purpose, methodology, and scope and limitation are discussed in this chapter.

The second chapter focuses on general introduction of the socio-historical and political background of Jeremiah by employing sociological method. Jeremiah's prophetic career can be classified into two, i.e., his earlier and later career. It also brings the political developments that took place around the AWA which have an impact on Israel and Judah.

The third chapter deals with an overview of covenant in the ancient and biblical world along with various scholarly opinions.

24 Lallawmzuala, "Hermeneutical Issues in the Old Testament," 120.

It examines terminology, meaning and definition of the covenant followed by how it was used in the AWA texts. It analyses scholarly stands, debates and discussions about the meaning and concept of covenant. It also gives the general understanding of the Bible, including a brief study of Noahic, Abrahamic, Mosaic, Davidic, the Deuteronomic covenant along with the new covenant. This chapter will be useful for analyzing the shift and development that occur in the old covenant to the new covenant.

The fourth chapter deals with a brief general survey of covenant motif in relation to new covenant in Jeremiah (with a particular focus on Jer 7:1-15; 7:21-26; 11:1-13; 24:4-7; 32:36-41), reading it through the lens of sociological approach to understand various covenant formula and covenant traditions. We cannot talk about a new covenant without talking first about the old covenant, about what has happened and why it is even necessary to speak about a new covenant. Jeremiah employed several covenant traditions such as Sinaitic Covenant as well as the Davidic, Abrahamic and Noahic covenants.

The fifth chapter examines Jer 31:31-34 in the light of literary-critical and other relevant methods. It shows that the selected text is a part of the book of comfort born out of the context of the exile. A general view of the form, structure and setting is briefly discussed to understand the historical context of the text. The new covenant has a concern for justice and righteousness. It has a concern to create new identity, inclusive community and equality with forgiveness, obedience and solidarity.

The sixth chapter deals with the new covenant motif and its implication for the tribal in Mizoram. This chapter examines the NT understanding of the new covenant. A general view on the NT usage is significant because the new covenant motif does not end in the OT, but continues through the NT as its fulfilment can be seen in Jesus who died on the cross. It also introduces the socio-economic, political and religious situation of the Mizo community. Furthermore, it highlights the ethical framework of the new covenant and effectively relates the ethical teaching of the new covenant to the context of the tribals in Mizo society.

The final chapter, the general conclusion, recapitulates some of the findings and observations of the research work. The concept of the new covenant has distinctive characters by creating new and inclusive community, justice and righteousness, equality, forgiveness, solidarity and communitarianism, obedience, comfort and hope. The ethical teachings of the new covenant have great implications for the contemporary community in Mizoram where there are many injustices, corruptions and oppressions. The chapter concludes that the Mizo traditional social ethics of *Zawlbuk* and *tlawmngaihna* as an ethical framework of the new covenant. The teaching of the new covenant in Jeremiah remains a powerful tool of liberation and emancipation of the tribal community in Mizoram.

Chapter 2

Socio-Historical and Political Background of Jeremiah

Introduction

In the previous chapter, the researcher has highlighted the main issue of the research work. It gives a clue that there are many issues and discussions regarding the covenantal understanding of Jeremiah particularly by the passage of the new covenant in Jer 31:31-34. On the one hand, some scholars suggest that there was nothing new in the new covenant; the old covenant was simply renewed. On the other hand, others claim that the new covenant was completely different from the old and it was wholly new. Thus, it attempts to examine the new covenant motif in the book of Jeremiah and tries to appropriate the ethical teaching of the new covenant for the socio-economic, political and religious situation of Mizoram and tries to draw the implication for the Church in Mizoram.

In this chapter, the researcher deals with the socio-historical and political background of Jeremiah by applying sociological method when needed. Hence, the study will answer some pivotal questions: What is the socio-historical and political context of Judah and Israel and what is the social setting of AWA during the period of Jeremiah? What is the significance of the Jeremiah's socio-historical and political background? How Jeremiah was impacted by the overall socio-political and historical and religious developments? How Jeremiah's thought pattern and theological thinking was influenced by the overall context?

2.1. Socio-Historical and Political Background

Jeremiah's context is primarily the seventh century ancient Israel.[25] He worked and noticed all the significant events of both the divided kingdoms of ancient Israel and Judah.[26] His dates correspond roughly to the last half-century of Israel's nationhood, i.e., 640-587 BCE. He survived the destruction of Jerusalem in 587 BCE and lived out the final years of his old age in Egypt, where he was taken by refugees who sought exile there. His life and ministry on behalf of Yahweh is the subject of the OT book bearing his name.[27] According to Jesurathnam, Jeremiah's prophetic period can be roughly classified into two major periods of his earlier and later career[28] along with the political developments that took around the AWA which will have an impact on Israel and Judah.

2.2. Jeremiah's Early Career (622-605 BCE)

We know very little about Jeremiah's early life aside from what is mentioned in the superscription to his book (Jer 1:1). Jeremiah

25 F. B. Huey, *Jeremiah, Lamentations: NAC,* vol. 16 (Nashville: Broadman & Holman Publishers, 1993), 19.

26 Jesurathnam, *Exploring Dalit Liberative Hermeneutics in India & The World*, 21.

27 Jack R. Lundbom, "Jeremiah (Prophet)," *ABD,* vol. 3 (New York: Doubleday, 1992): 684.

28 Lundbom, "Jeremiah (Prophet)," *ABD*: 685; Thompson, *The Book of Jeremiah, NICOT,* 10; Jesurathnam, *Exploring Dalit Liberative Hermeneutics in India & the World*, 22-31.

was born the son of Hilkiah, a priest at Anathoth.[29] He received his prophetic vocation in the thirteenth year of King Josiah (640-609 BCE, Jer 1:2; 25:3) that falls in 627 BCE, while he was a young man.[30] Jeremiah's call is to be a prophet to the nations. His life's work is *to pluck up and to break down...To build and to plant* (Jer 1:10). Jeremiah accepts the call in 622 BCE after the temple scroll was found.[31] God informed Jeremiah that he had consecrated and appointed him before birth (Jer 1:4–5). He was promised protection (Jer 1:18) and deliverance (Jer 1:8) despite opposition (Jer 1:19). God touched his mouth, signifying divine inspiration of God's words, and gave the sign of a branch from an almond tree, explaining that the Lord is watching. The third sign was the boiling pot (Jer 1:13) facing from the north, picturing the source and fury of impending disaster.[32] Thus, the tone of Jeremiah's life ministry was set by judgment, disaster, danger, defeat, and impending death for the nation.

2.2.1. Josianic Reformation from 622 BCE

The messages given by Jeremiah during his first five years of ministry may have been instrumental in the great revival of 622 BCE. Jesurathnam rightly remarks,

> Jeremiah was an ardent supporter of Josianic reform program which may have begun in the year 622 BCE

---

29 Lundbom, "Jeremiah (Prophet)," *ABD*: 686.

30 W. L. Holladay suggests that thirteenth year of Josiah was the date of Jeremiah's birth rather than the beginning of his prophetic career. See W. L. Holladay, *Jeremiah: Spokesman Out of Time* (Philadelphia: United Church Press, 1974), 18-22. J. P. Hyatt also proposed this view. See Hyatt, "The book of Jeremiah," *IB*, 5. See J. R. Lundbom, *Jeremiah 1-20, AB* (New York: Doubleday, 1999), 107-109. Overholt comes to the conclusion that it is more reasonable to take the traditional understanding of 627 BCE as the date of Jeremiah's call. See T. W. Overholt, "Some Reflections on the Date of Jeremiah's Call," *CBQ* 33 (1971): 184.

31 Lundbom, "Jeremiah (Prophet)," *ABD*: 686.

32 Walter A. Elwell & Philip Wesley Comfort, *Tyndale Bible Dictionary* (Wheaton, Illinois: Tyndale House Publishers, 2001), 680.

> during which time Jeremiah was actively involved in his prophetic ministry. In fact, the reform program of Josiah was at the center of Jeremiah's preaching.[33]

The account of Josiah's reform is given in 2 Kings 22-23 and 2 Chr 34-35. The accounts differ somewhat[34] and the reform no doubt took some time. J. A. Thompson rightly observed that "the reform was comprehensive and far-reaching. But, there were other factors than the religious one. The reform was a principal expression of a resurgent nationalism. Political unification and cultic unification went hand in hand."[35] Patrick D. Miller also described,

> The reform, however, was not only political endeavor. The discovery of a law book while the Temple was being renovated, itself a part of Josiah's reforming activity, gave significant impetus to the impulse for reform. There is no reason to doubt the judgment of Kings that Josiah was a committed Yahwist as well as an assertive nationalist.[36]

Jeremiah supported the nationalistic and Yahwistic reform program of Josiah. For this reason, he had to face some consequences recorded in his experiences (Jer 11:18-12:6) and for supporting the centralized worship in Jerusalem along with Josiah (Jer 3:12-14; 31:2-14), because the reform program virtually means to close down Anathoth sanctuary. Jeremiah's preaching on obedience to the covenant (Jer 11:1-8) and his call for a more

---

33 Jesurathnam, *Exploring Dalit Liberative Hermeneutics in India & the World*, 23.

34 Bustenay Oded, "Judah and the Exile," *Israelite and Judaean History*, ed. John H. Hayes and J. Maxwell Miller (London: SCM Press Ltd., 1977), 460.

35 Thompson, *The Book of Jeremiah, NICOT,* 19.

36 Patrick D. Miller, "The Book of Jeremiah: Introduction, Commentary, and Reflections," *NIB,* vol. IV (Nashville: Abingdon Press, 2001): 556.

rigorous practice of Sabbath observance (Jer 17:19-27) also fit well into the period after 622 BCE.[37]

2.2.2. Historical Setting of AWA at the Time of Jeremiah

Jeremiah was born and grew into the world of tumultuous change and disturbing political context of the AWA. The long reign of Manasseh came to an end in 642 BCE. Assyria's power began to wane after the death of Ashurbanipal in 627 BCE at the year in which Jeremiah began his career as a prophet.[38] Babylon was in open revolt and in 626 BCE, Nabopolassar defeated the Assyrian army outside the city of Babylon and declared himself king of Babylon. Assyria was now on the defensive and Nineveh fell in 612 BCE. In 609 BCE, Egypt went to Assyria's aid in the attempt to retake Haran but the mission failed. The Babylonians were now in control of all of Mesopotamia.[39]

During the reign of Josiah (638-609 BCE) the kingdom of Judah had experienced some kind of revival. This was mainly due to the weakness of Assyria. The Bible relates that Pharaoh Neco II clashed with king Josiah at Meggido and killed him (2 Kings 23:29; 2 Chr 35:20).[40] The struggle between Egypt and Babylon for hegemony in Syro-Palestine continued for some time. And by 605 BCE, the Egyptian-Assyrian coalition failed to counter Babylon's strength. Thus, with Nebuchadnezzar's defeat of the Egyptians at Carchemish (Jer 46), Assyrian power was at an end.[41]

On Josiah's death, his son Jehoahaz became king. After three months he was summoned to Riblah by Necho, and sent in bonds to Egypt. His brother Eliakim, assuming the throne name Jehoiakim, was set in his place as an Egyptian vassal. Judah was laid under

37 Jesurathnam, *Exploring Dalit Liberative Hermeneutics in India & the World*, 23-24.

38 Thompson, *The Book of Jeremiah, NICOT*, 14.

39 Lundbom, "Jeremiah (Prophet)," *ABD*: 685.

40 P. A. Beaulieu, "History of Israel 6: Babylonian Period," *Dictionary of the Old Testament: Historical Books*, eds. Bill T. Arnold and H. G. M. Williamson (Illinois: InterVarsity Press, 2005), 479.

41 Miller, "The Book of Jeremiah," *NIB*: 557.

heavy tribute.[42] However, he revolted at the first sign of weakness on Babylon's part. Jehoiakim died and his son, Jehoiachin, assumed the throne.[43] The Babylonians took Jehoiachin prisoner and put Josiah's third son, Zedekiah, on the throne. But, Zedekiah also was determined to follow a policy of independence. He too revolted, counting on help from Egypt that never materialized.[44]

2.2.3. Post-Josianic Reform Period of Jeremiah's Ministry

The years from 609 to 605 BCE were difficult for the prophet. When Necho installed Jehoiakim, the political climate in Jerusalem changed.[45] The year 605 BCE was pivotal for the nation and for Jeremiah personally. The battle of Carchemish left Egypt weakened and Babylon became the new power in world affairs. Jeremiah addressed the Egyptian defeat with an oracle (Jer 46:2-12). Jeremiah also decided in this year to prepare the first written scroll of his oracles, and that signaled the end of his early career. After the scroll was read publicly, Jeremiah and Baruch were forced to go into hiding, for they were now in direct conflict with the king (Jer 36).[46]

2.3. Jeremiah's Later Career (604-586 BCE)

These years are remarkably well documented. According to Lundbom, "There are 2 periods of roughly 7 years each, 604-597 BCE, and 594-588 BCE, during which we have no definite knowledge of Jeremiah's activities." It is unlikely that Jeremiah had any public ministry during Jehoiakim's remaining years. He

---

42 Thompson, *The Book of Jeremiah*, *NICOT*, 22-23.

43 Anthony R. Ceresko, *The Old Testament: A Liberation Perspective* (Bangalore: St. Paul, 1993), 274.

44 Ceresko, *The Old Testament: A Liberation Perspective*, 274.

45 Jesurathnam, *Exploring Dalit Liberative Hermeneutics in India & the World*, 23-24.

46 Lundbom, "Jeremiah (Prophet)," *ABD*: 688-689.

certainly had nothing good to say about this king.[47] Jehoiakim was no worthy successor of his father, but a petty tyrant unfit to rule.[48]

2.3.1. Events Related to the 597 BCE

Jerusalem fell into Babylonian hands on March 15/16, 597 BCE.[49] When the city surrendered to Nebuchadnezzar in 597 BCE, Jeremiah was again actively speaking the divine word and articulating as well the expressions of grief which were widespread (Jer 10:17-25; 13:15-27). His message to the departing exiles was hopeful yet bittersweet (Jer 31:21-22). He said Jehoiachin would not return home, nor would any of his offspring sit on David's throne (Jer 22:24-30).[50]

Nebuchadnezzar put Zedekiah on the throne before departing from Jerusalem. The date of the prose in the book indicates that Jeremiah was active during the first four years of Zedekiah's reign (597-594/3 BCE) and then again when Jerusalem was under siege for the last time in 588-587 BCE. During Zedekiah's middle years, Jeremiah was perhaps addressing certain foreign nations with oracles (Jer 48–51) in addition to writing more scrolls with Baruch.[51]

2.3.2. Final Events Related to the Destruction of Jerusalem and the Temple

The final years of Judah were turbulent and filled with disastrous events leading to the deportation of cream of the population to Babylon as exiles. The deportation of 597 BCE was significant for it removed many of Judah's key personnel.[52] Jeremiah was

47 Lundbom, "Jeremiah (Prophet)," *ABD*: 689.

48 John Bright, *A History of Israel,* Third Ed. (London: SCM Press Ltd, 1964), 325-326.

49 Herrmann Siegfried, *A History of Israel in Old Testament Times (*London: SCM Press Ltd, 1975), 250.

50 Lundbom, "Jeremiah (Prophet)," *ABD*: 689.

51 Lundbom, "Jeremiah (Prophet)," *ABD*: 689.

52 The figures in 2 Kings 24:14,16 are 10,000 and 8,000, while Jer. 52:58 gives 3023. It was not certain of how the count was made. The first two

well aware of the final events prior to the destruction and the Babylonian exile. A rebellion in Babylon in 595 BCE seems to have stirred hopes of Judah's breaking free of Babylonian domination.[53] Jerusalem and its Temple were destroyed after the Temple was looted. Many of the leaders were executed, and many people were taken into exile in Babylon. Zedekiah was forced to watch his sons being executed before the Babylonians put out his eyes and dragged him off to Babylon.[54]

A number of Judeans were left behind, including Jeremiah. The Babylonians appointed Gedaliah as governor of Judah. Unfortunately, Gedaliah was assassinated by Ishmael.[55] Fearful of Babylonian retaliation, some of the remaining leaders ignored Jeremiah's counsel to stay put and insisted on fleeing to Egypt, taking Jeremiah and his scribe Baruch with them (Jer 43). We last hear him preaching a sermon against the Judean refugees in Egypt, accusing them of idolatry and abandoning their allegiance to the Lord of Israel (Jer 44).[56]

2.3.3. After 586 BCE

Jeremiah reiterated Yahweh's judgment upon that nation (Jer 43:8-13). His message to expatriate Jews was essentially what it had been back in Jerusalem some years earlier (Jer 44). These people, however, had a different view of things. They said the destruction of Jerusalem came about because worship of the Queen of Heaven was discontinued. Jeremiah assures Yahweh will have the last word. This remnant in Egypt will die though it came there to live. We hear no more from Jeremiah and the Bible does not

---

are round figure. The third may represent males only, or the number of those who survived. Thompson, *The Book of Jeremiah*, *NICOT*, 22-23; see also Niels Peter Lemche, *Ancient Israel: A New History of Israelite Society* (Sheffield: JSOT Press, 1990), 175-176.

53 Lundbom, "Jeremiah (Prophet)," *ABD*: 689.

54 Miller, "The Book of Jeremiah," *NIB*: 559-560.

55 Beaulieu, "History of Israel 6: Babylonian Period," 483.

56 Miller, "The Book of Jeremiah," *NIB*: 559-560.

mention his death. Later sources contain conflicting reports about martyrdom and a natural death in Egypt.[57]

2.4. Significance of Jeremiah's Socio-Historical Context

Walter Brueggemann[58] identified three elements that are constitutive of this covenantal understanding of historical reality, such as:

2.4.1. The governing paradigm for the tradition of Jeremiah is Israel's with Yahweh, rooted in the memories and mandates of the Sinai tradition. That covenant taught that the sovereign God of Israel required obedience to covenant stipulations about social practice and power. Disobedience to those covenant stipulations would result in heavy sanctions that would be experienced as death or displacement. This paradigm of covenant indicates that Jeremiah is in important ways related to and derived from the traditions of Deuteronomy.[59] Therefore, Jeremiah reaffirms what was stated by the Deuteronomy and strictly demands that the people should adhere to the Sinai covenantal stipulations.

2.4.2. A clear evidence how Jeremiah departs from Deuteronomic theology is that he affirms another theological claim, i.e., the pathos of Yahweh, along with the paradigm of covenant. Brueggemann asserts:[60]

> The mediation of the claims of covenant through the surprising power of Yahweh's pathos permits the book

57 Lundbom, "Jeremiah (Prophet)," *ABD*: 690.

58 Brueggemann, *A Commentary on Jeremiah: Exile and Homecoming*, 3-7.

59 John Bright, "The Date of the Prose Sermons of Jeremiah," *A Prophet to the Nations: Essays in Jeremiah Studies*, eds. Leo G. Perdue and Brian W. Kovacs (Winona Lake, Indiana: Eisenbraunts, 1984): 193-212; J. Philip Hyatt, "The Deuteronomic Edition of Jeremiah," *A Prophet to the Nations: Essays in Jeremiah Studies*, eds. Leo G. Perdue and Brian W. Kovacs (Winona Lake, Indiana: Eisenbraunts, 1984): 247-267; Robert P. Carroll, *From Chaos to Covenant: Prophecy in the Book of Jeremiah* (New York: Crossroad, 1981), 85.

60 Brueggemann, *A Commentary on Jeremiah: Exile and Homecoming*, 5-6.

> of Jeremiah to move beyond the crisis of exile and death in 7th and 6th centuries to envision a newness. The move beyond covenantal sanction is unwarranted, but the move is possible because of God's magisterial freedom, through which God can and does act beyond warrants. Jeremiah's discernment and articulation of the freedom and pathos of Yahweh enables the poet to break out of the tight categories of covenantal sanctions and move to an articulation of hope.

Thus, Jeremiah did not just rely on Deuteronomic scheme, but moved beyond the mechanical acts of retribution.

2.4.3. Another element of the theology of the book of Jeremiah is the royal-temple ideology of Jerusalem. The royal-temple ideology was the undergirding principle that every section of the royal house and the priesthood that supported the royal house talked about at the time of Jeremiah. But Jeremiah countered the majority opinion by deconstructing the false and presumptuous notions of royal-temple ideology that was responsible for the downfall of Judah.[61] Thus, it is evident that Jeremiah took pain in reinterpreting some of age-old traditions of royal-temple ideology.[62]

Therefore, the book of Jeremiah: 1) reinterprets the events of *Realpolitik* through the categories of covenantal obligation and covenantal sanctions. 2) disrupts the claims of the covenantal (Deuteronomic) pattern of obligation and sanction by a disclosure of the pathos of God that will not be contained in the tradition of covenant, and 3) utilizes the combination of covenantal motifs and divine pathos to critique and reject the claims of the royal-temple ideology.[63]

61 Jesurathnam, *Exploring Dalit Liberative Hermeneutics in India & the World*, 33.

62 Brueggemann, *A Commentary on Jeremiah: Exile and Homecoming,* 7.

63 Brueggemann, *A Commentary on Jeremiah: Exile and Homecoming,* 7.

Conclusion

On the basis of the above discussion, we can recapitulate the importance of Jeremiah's socio-political and historical background as follows:

First, Jeremiah was impacted by the overall socio-political and historical and religious developments. Therefore, his thought pattern and theological thinking are influenced by the overall context. He makes use of the combination of covenantal motifs, divine pathos to critique and subvert the extraordinary claims of royal-temple ideology. He talks about the triumph as well as disaster in unequivocal terms for the welfare of the community of Judah. Jesurathnam rightly points out that Jeremiah's message also puts us in a grip of ideology that there cannot be any permanent security in any ideology, nationalism, patriotism, ritual, institution, ancestry, history or whatever that can be of an exclusive claim.[64] Therefore, the socio-historical and political context of Jeremiah points out to the concreteness of the prophetic message that will not only address the crisis situation but also leads us to look forward in hope.

Second, Jeremiah's context is crucial because he witnessed all the significant events of both the divided kingdoms of ancient Israel and Judah. He also noticed the turmoil and disturbing political situation of the AWA. Therefore the book of Jeremiah is reflective of and responsive to the historical crisis that happened during his time. Thus, the tone of his preaching was set by judgment, disaster, danger, defeats, and impending death for the nation.

Third, the socio-political and historical context of Jeremiah clearly shows that Jeremiah was not in search of some political answers for the crises situation, rather return to the basic covenant stipulations that the community had lost in their faith journey. It was also the demand of Yahweh that the people should return to the covenantal traditions of faith so that their aspirations, hopes and the laments and frustrations will be addressed. It was

64 Jesurathnam, *Exploring Dalit Liberative Hermeneutics in India & the World*, 35.

also the demand from the God of Israelites that they should uncompromisingly recognize Yahweh's sovereignty in the midst of other seemingly powerful deities that Israelites encountered.[65]

Fourth, the message of Jeremiah *to pluck and to pull down, to destroy and to overthrow, to build and to plant* (Jer 1:10) envisages the overthrowing of the unjust and corrupt structures of the society and the building up of a new society of justice and righteousness. The idea of justice and righteousness is clearly seen in the Temple Sermon in Jer 7:1-5 and 26:1-24.

Fifth, as mentioned above, the painful experience around 587 BCE made clear the inadequacy of both the old covenant theology and the royal-temple theology. The new circumstances around 587 BCE required a new theological assertion.[66] Therefore, Jeremiah does not preach his message in a political vacuum; rather ends his message with a reconstruction of new communities as per the covenant stipulations set by Yahweh.[67] God will make new covenant with them so that their hope will be restored. God will create new community and inclusive community in the midst of social evils, corruption, deceit, injustice and immorality that are rampant during the period of Jeremiah.

65 Jesurathnam, *Exploring Dalit Liberative Hermeneutics in India & the World*, 31.

66 Brueggemann, *A Commentary on Jeremiah: Exile and Homecoming*, 6.

67 Jesurathnam, *Exploring Dalit Liberative Hermeneutics in India & the World*, 35.

Chapter 3

Covenant in the Ancient and Biblical World Etymological and Related Significant Concerns

Introduction

In the previous chapter, we discussed that Jeremiah was impacted by the overall socio-political, historical and religious developments and his thought pattern and theological thinking is influenced by the overall context. It succinctly dealt with the significance of the background studies that the idea of covenant can be seen throughout the history of Jeremiah and the concept of covenant particularly the new covenant is the main emphasis of the prophet. Thus, there are several issues which will be dealt with in this chapter. What exactly is the term and meaning of covenant? What are the different kinds of covenant mentioned in the Bible? How Jeremiah's, AWA's and other covenant contexts are similar or different? How far the concept of covenant in the Bible is related to the AWA's understanding? Whether Covenant is determined by the presence of *bĕrît* or the overall sense of the term in the sense of relationship between God and the people? Is there any reference to the new covenant elsewhere in the Bible apart from Jeremiah?

3.1. Etymology of *bĕrît* (בְּרִית)

The word *bĕrît* (286 occurrences) is translated as *covenant* in the OT and in Greek it is rendered as: διαθηκη and in Vulgate it is *Testamentum* or *pactum*.[68] The etymology of *bĕrît* is uncertain. Some of the derivations that have been suggested by different scholars are hereunder:

3.1.1. *Bĕrît* is a feminine noun from the root hrb, which means *to eat, to cut, to dine* (cf. 2 Sam 3:35; 12:17; 13:5,6,10). It refers to the festive meal accompanying the covenant ceremony[69] indicating a contract or agreement between persons and covenant between God and humankind.[70] But, Quell suggests that the feminine noun tyrb emerged from hyrb, which also means *food or eat* in 2 Sam.13:6,10.[71]

3.1.2. For some scholars like Delitzch and Albright, *bĕrît* is also identical with Akkadian *birit* and *biritu* meaning *between, among or fetter.*[72] Weinfeld[73] remarks that "the most plausible solution seems to be the one that associates *bĕrît* with the Akkadian *biritu*

68 George E. Mendenhall, "Covenant" *IDB*, vol. I., ed. George Arthur Buttrick, et al. (Nashville: Abingdon Press, 1962): 715.

69 Ludwig Koehler, "Problems in the Study of the Language of the Old Testament," *JSS* 1/1, (January, 1956): 6.

70 Ludwig Koehler and Walter Baumgartner, *The Hebrew and Aramaic Lexicon of the Old Testament*, vol. I, trans. and ed. M. E. J. Richardson (New York: E. J. Brill, 1994), 157-156.

71 C. D. Jathana, "The Covenant and Covenant Making in Pentateuch," *BTF* 3/1 (Jan-June, 1969): 34.

72 Weinfeld, "בְּרִית," *TDOT*, vol. II, eds. G. Johannes Botterweck and Helmer Ringgren, trans. John T. Willis (Grand Rapids: William B. Eerdmans Publishing Company, 1977): 254-255. Also see, Jathana, "The Covenant and Covenant Making in Pentateuch," *BTF*: 35.

73 Weinfeld,"בְּרִית," *TDOT*: 255.

which means *clasp, fetter*. This is supported by the Akkadian and Hittite terms for *treaty*.[74]

3.1.3. E. Kutsch, on the other hand, suggested the derivation of *bĕrît* from hrb from the Akkadian root *baru* with the basic meaning *to look for, or choose*. According to Kutsch, the meaning of this verb developed into *determining or fixing*.[75] P. C. Mathew accuses Kutsch[76] of a misleading etymological study of *bĕrît*.[77]

James Barr argued that none of these theories are completely satisfying because scholars make too much of etymology.[78] C. D. Jathana may also be right when he says that there are a number of instances where words have lost their original meaning and have come to be used in a sense widely divergent from the form from which they are derived.[79] Therefore, what is more important is to exhibit the underlying theological significance of the covenant which involve the meaning and definition of the covenant.

3.2. Meaning of Covenant

Weinfeld does not think that the aspect of the Akkadian word *riksu* gives that idea. He believes that the covenant is commanded by a superior party on his subordinate or vassal.[80] Behm, following

74 Weinfeld, "בְּרִית," *TDOT*: 255.

75 He further says that the main evidence for this etymology comes from the word hzx/ twzx, which is parallel to בְּרִית in Isaiah 28:15,18. Weinfeld, "בְּרִית," *TDOT*: 255; also see E. Kutch "בְּרִית," *Theological Lexicon of the Old Testament,* vol. I, eds. Ernst Jenni and Claus Westermann (Peabody: Hendrickson Publishers, Inc., 1997), 257.

76 P. C. Mathew, *Berith: The Semitic Concept of Divine Human Relationship* (Kottayam: Ashram Press, 1987), 222. See also Paul Kalluveettil, *Declaration and Covenant: A Comprehensive Review of Covenant Formulae from the Old Testament and the Ancient Near East* (Rome: Biblical Institute Press, 1982), 9-11.

77 Mathew, *Berith*, 241.

78 James Barr, *The Semantic Biblical Language* (Glasgow: Oxford University Press, 1961), 107.

79 Jathana, "The Covenant and Covenant Making in Pentateuch," *BTF*: 36.

80 Martin Noth, *The Laws in the Pentateuch and Other Studies*, trans. D. R. Ap-Thomas (Edinburgh and London: Oliver & Boyd, 1967), 38.

Noth,[81] thinks that the word *bĕrît* is identical with the Akkadian preposition *birit*, which means *between or among*. According to Behm, the general meaning of covenant is usually taken as mutual agreement between two parties. Thus, most generally accepted is the derivation of *bĕrît* from the Akkadian *biritu*, which means *clasp or fetter*. In the midst such debate, Mendenhall argues that the original meaning was lost in antiquity before the time of Moses, and had simply become a technical term.[82]

3.2.1. Defining Covenant

The OT scholars have endeavoured to rediscover the significance of the covenant relationship and its theological relevance from different angles.

According to Mendenhall and Gary A. Herion, a covenant is an agreement between two parties in which one or both make promises under oath to perform or refrain from certain actions stipulated in advance…it is the instrument constituting the rule of God and it is therefore a valuable lens through which one can recognize and appreciate the biblical ideal of religious community.[83] Kraetzschmar defines *bĕrît* as a cultic act, through which in a ceremonial way obligations or stipulations are made binding. Its significance comes through the art of binding the obligations and on account of this it is called covenant, contract, solemn promise, obligation, oath.[84] Pedersen agrees *bĕrît* as *contract* or *treaty* of a bilateral character. He explains the covenant relationship as *psychic community*, a covenant of kin

81 Noth, *The Laws in the Pentateuch and Other Studies*, 38.

82 Mendenhall, "Covenant" *IDB:* 716.

83 George E. Mendenhall and Gary A. Herion, "Covenant," *ABD*, vol. I, eds. David Noel Freedman, et al. (London: Doubleday, 1992): 1179.

84 Klaus Baltzer, *The Covenant Formulary: In Old Testament, Jewish, and Early Christian Writings*, trans. David E. Green (Oxford: Basil Blackwell, 1971), 3.

and friendship, a community of souls.[85] Eichrodt[86] and Kohler[87] also consider *bĕrît* as bilateral. Eichrodt firmly declares:[88]

> ...the use of the covenant concept in secular life argues that the religious *bĕrît* too was always regarded as a bilateral relationship; for, even though the burden is most unequally distributed between the two contracting parties, this makes no difference to the fact that the relationship is still essentially two-sided.

Begrich shows that the ancient concept of *bĕrît* was *unilateral*, the superior party granting the covenant relationship to the inferior party (Jos 9:6). It is the superior party who takes the initiative, presents cloth or weapons, arranges the meal, takes the oath, binds to the promise and assures *shalom,* the content of the covenant.[89] N. K. Gottwald defines covenant as a way of symbolizing the ground and origin of the proper ordering of Israel's communal life, the covenant is a total religio-political reality.[90] Perhaps Jathana's definition may well be fitting. According to him, covenant relationship between God and his people as "a significant factor dominating the whole religious, social, economic and political life of the people of God."[91]

---

85 Johs. Pedersen, *Israel: Its Life and Culture*, vols. I & II (London: Oxford University Press, 1959), 271.

86 Walther Eichrodt, *Theology of the Old Testament*, vol. I, trans. J. A. Baker (Philadelphia: The Westminster Press, 1960), 37.

87 Lugwig Kohler, *Old Testament Theology*, trans. A. S. Todd (Philadelphia: The Westminster Press, 1957), 622.

88 Eichrodt, *Theology of the Old Testament I*, 37.

89 Ralph L. Smith, *Old Testament Theology: Its History, Method, and Message* (Nashville: Broadman & Holman Publishers, 1993), 146.

90 Norman K. Gottwald, *The Hebrew Bible: A Socio-Literary Introduction* (Philadelphia: Fortress Press, 1987), 204.

91 Jathana, "The Covenant and Covenant Making in Pentateuch," *BTF*: 27.

3.3. Covenant in the AWA Texts

Jathana lists out several texts in the AWA which relates to covenant including the Amarna texts, the Ugaritic texts and the Mari texts.[92] We also find the Mesopotamian context of the Hittite treaties such as parity and suzerain-vassal treaties. Parity treaty is a treaty made between two equal partners. Seven common elements are normally recognized in this treaty. They are: i) mutual titulature; ii) history of the past relations; iii) affirmation of brotherhood; iv) stipulations; v) list of divine utterances; vi) curses and blessings; vii) addendum concerning the fugitives.[93] For instance we see this goodwill between the Hittites and Egyptians in the following text:

> "…And as for (the relationship of) the land of Egypt with Hatti land, they are at peace and brothers like us forever."[94]

In Suzerain-vassal treaty, the suzerain always demands certain obligations from vassal and there are six common elements present in this type of treaty as follows: i) Preamble introducing the sovereign; ii) The historical prologue describing previous relations between the contracting parties; iii) The stipulations which outlinc the nature of the community formed by the covenant; iv) The document clause providing for preservation and regular re-reading of the treaty; v) The list of gods who witnessed the treaty; vi) The curse and blessing formula, curses depending upon infidelity and blessing upon fidelity to the covenant.[95]

---

92 Jathana, "The Covenant and Covenant Making in Pentateuch," *BTF*: 42.

93 For instance, there was a treaty made between a Hittite king Hattiusilis III and the Egyptian king Ramses II. Dennis J. McCarthy, *Treaty and Covenant: A Study in Form in the Ancient Oriental Documents and in the Old Testament* (Rome: Pontifical Biblical Institute, 1963), 25. Jesurathnam, *Old Testament Theology: History, Issues, and Perspectives*, 218-219.

94 James B. Pitchard, *Ancient Near Eastern Texts* (Princeton: Princeton University Press, 1950), 202.

95 Mendenhall, "Covenant," *IDB*: 714-716.

3.4. Convergence and Divergence between OT Covenant and AWA Treaties

E. Bickermann seems to have been the first scholar to notice a possible analogy between the treaties of the Hittite kings and their vassals and the covenant relationship between Yahweh and Israel.[96] George Mendenhall argued that the Hittite treaty form was an early source of the OT's idea of covenant. He argued that the tribes of Israel were not bound together by blood-ties but by a covenant based on religion and modelled after the suzerainty treaty by which the great Hittite king bound his vassals to faithfulness and obedience to himself.[97] McCarthy also concluded that the Israelite covenant form resembled that of the Hittite treaty form.[98]

The convergence between OT covenant and AWA treaties, according to scholars, are as follows: One, a preamble, the identification of the great king is very much similar to Ex 20: *I am Yahweh your God.* Two, the claim of suzerains upon the exclusive loyalty and subservience of their vassals, characteristic of the treaties, has been seen as the prototype of the corresponding claim of Yahweh upon Israel's exclusive worship and service in the first commandment of the decalogue. Three, curse formula in the OT texts, notably in Deut 28, have been regarded as the result of direct borrowing from lists of such curses in treaty documents. Four, the vassal treaties have been regarded as the source or background of the nature and content of Yahweh's *rīb lawsuit* with Israel, exemplified in a number of texts in the OT (e.g. Deut 32; Is 1:2-3; 10-20; Jer 2:5-13; etc).[99]

However, scholars have drawn various criticisms of the convergence between AWA Treaties and the covenant texts of the OT. Nicholson has presented some forceful arguments and asserts that the parallels to the suzerainty treaty *yielded little that is of*

96 Ernest W. Nicholson, *God and His People: Covenant and Theology in the Old Testament* (Oxford: Clarendon Press, 1986), 57.

97 Smith, *Old Testament Theology*, 140.

98 McCarthy, *Treaty and Covenant*, 174.

99 Nicholson, *God and His People*, 63.

value. The reasons for his conclusion are: One, Deuteronomy is not a legal document in the sense that the treaties are. Second, it is not treaty-like in its manner of presentation; rather it is a valedictory speech of Moses. Third, its laws deal with many matters not strictly pertinent to the suzerain-vassal relationship. Fourth, the fact that Deuteronomy contains two prologues unlike anything found in treaties. Fifth, conspicuously absent is the designation of *Yahweh as King*.[100] Therefore, there are similarities as well as dissimilarities between OT covenant and AWA treaties.

3.5. The Covenant Relationship

With a view of the concept that whether covenant is determined by the presence of *bĕrît* or the overall sense of the term in the sense of relationship between God and the people, Eichrodt rightly remarked that covenant is the concept in which Israelite thought gave definitive expression to the binding of the people of God and by means of which they established firmly from the start. Thus, for him, covenant is determined by the basis of the relationship with God and the covenant-union between Yahweh and Israel is an original element in all sources. The presence of *bĕrît* itself is not the determining factor because even where the covenant is not explicitly mentioned the spiritual premises of the covenant relationship with God are manifestly present.[101]

3.6. Recent Trends in the Study of the Covenant

A lively debate has developed among OT scholars over the meaning of the word *bĕrît*. Kutsch and Perlitt seemed to turn scholars' direction from the *treaty form* of the covenant to that of a *theological idea*. Ernst Kutsch conducted a thorough study of the contexts of the various uses of the word *bĕrît* in the OT. He concluded that the primary meaning of the word *bĕrît* was *obligation*. It never means a relationship, an alliance, or a covenant, but always an obligation.[102]

---

100 Nicholson, *God and His People*, 63.

101 Eichrodt, *Theology of the Old Testament I*, 36-37.

102 Smith, *Old Testament Theology*, 147.

3.6.1. The Covenant Silence in the Eight Century Prophets

Lothar Perlitt dated the *full-blown* idea of the covenant between Yahweh and Israel in the post-Exilic period.[103] He attacked the form-critical approach of Mendenhall and the whole comparative religions approach to the study of *bĕrît*. Perlitt insisted against Eichrodt that the theology of covenant must be tied inseparably to the actual usage of the term *bĕrît*. He reverted to the old Wellhausen view that all references to *bĕrît* in the OT are late-no earlier than the Deuteronomic materials. Every mention of a *bĕrît* in the Sinai accounts is eliminated by literary-critical procedures.[104] For him, the account of Yahweh's *bĕrît* with Abraham in Genesis 15 in its present form was an early Deuteronomic document to be dated at the beginning of the seventh century.[105]

For Perlitt, Hebrew *bĕrît* is given a meaning different from the conventional translation *covenant*. Following E. Kutsch's work, he asserts that *bĕrît* refers basically not to a relationship; rather the basic meaning is *obligation*, which one may take oneself or impose on another. He goes on to propose a history of *bĕrît* as a theological concept in the OT with and by the Deuteronomic school.[106] According to him, covenant theology arose when the Yahweh-Israel relationship was seriously challenged.[107] He believes that the covenant theology in the OT is a late fruit of Israelite belief which is due to the theological creativity of the Deuteronomistic movement and epoch. This then explains the *covenant silence* in the prophets of the 8th century.[108] Perlitt

103 Smith, *Old Testament Theology*, 145.

104 Smith, *Old Testament Theology*, 147.

105 Walther Zimmerli, "The History of Israelite Religion," *Tradition and Interpretation*, ed. G. W. Anderson, (Philadelphia: Fortress Press, 1979): 379-380.

106 Dennis J. McCarthy, review of *Bundestheologies im Alten Testament*, by Lothar Perlitt, *Biblica* 53/1 (1972): 110-111.

107 Peter J. Kearney, review of *Bundestheologies im Alten Testament*, by Lothar Perlitt, *CBQ* 34 (1972): 525.

108 Gerhard Hasel, *Old Testament Theology: Basic Issues in the Current Debates,* revised edition (Grand Rapids: William B. Eerdmans Publishing

asserts, "If we go back beyond this time (7th and 6th centuries BCE), we come up against the silence of the 8th century prophets regarding the covenant."[109]

However, scholars like E.W. Nicholson observed Perlitt's work and concluded that 'the covenant as a full-blown theory was a late arrival in Israel is seen to be substantially vindicated, but Perlitt is shown to have been on shaky ground in insisting that it is so late as to have been completely unknown to the eight-century prophets. Rather, the idea emerged at some point during the late monarchical period.'[110] According to Martin J. Buss, Perlitt seems to overlook repeatedly that all historical knowledge is uncertain, so lack of proof of a theory does not prove its opposite. So odd handling of historical criticism is lamentable.[111] J. J. Roberts saw the discussion of Perlitt as a return to a narrow, biblically based discussion of the covenant on a simple syntactical study of a single Hebrew word. Roberts thought that the avoidance of comparative AWA materials is *a false step*.[112]

One will agree with Perlitt that his influential work had the effect of bringing the origins of the covenant idea down to a much later period against the consensus view from the 1920s to the 1960s. The way how he shifted the emphasis of covenant from the institutional to the theological idea is also remarkable.

Co., 1979), 140.

109 Lothar Perlitt, "Covenant," *The Encyclopedia of Christianity*, vol. 1, ed. Erwin Fahlbusch et al. (Grand Rapids, Michigan: William B. Eerdmans Publishing Company, 1997), 710.

110 Nicholson, *God and His People*, vi.

111 Martin J. Buss, review of *Bundestheologies im Alten Testament*, by Lothar Perlitt, *JBL* 90/2 (1971), 211.

112 J. J. Roberts, "Ancient Near Eastern Environment," *The Hebrew Bible and Its Modern Interpreters*, ed. Knight and Tucker (Philadelphia: Fortress Press, 1985), 93-94.

3.7. Covenant in the Bible

3.7.1. The Noahic Covenant

The first covenant is made by God to Noah, his descendants, and with all future humanity, including all other living creatures (Gen 6:18; 9:8-17). The covenant is a one-sided commitment on God's part, by which God undertakes never to flood the earth and thus destroy life on earth. Dyrness opines that the scope of this promise is not limited to Noah and his seed, but is universal.[113] John Goldingay observes that:

> The covenant is an *everlasting* one. As long as human life continues on earth, this covenant commitment will hold. The Noah covenant is thus significant for all humanity throughout the ages. It guarantees the security of human and animal creation from divine destruction.[114]

3.7.2. The Abrahamic and Davidic Covenant

Both the Abrahamic and Davidic covenants belong to the category of promissory covenant. In the case of Abraham it is God's promise of land and in David's case it is the promise of dynasty. In the case of Abraham the covenant is explained in two different traditions: J (Gen 15) and P (Gen 17:1-14). In the Abrahamic covenant (Gen 12; 15; 17) God promised Abraham a great name, a great nation and a great land.[115] In the Davidic covenant God made a promise

---

113 William Dyrness, *Themes of the Old Testament Theology* (Illinois: Intervarsity Press, 1979), 117.

114 John Goldingay, "Covenant, OT and NT," *NIDB*, vol. 1, ed. K. D. Sekenfeld et al. (Nashville: Abingdon Press, 2006): 768.

115 T. Rata, "Covenant," *Dictionary of the Old Testament Prophets*, eds. Mark J. Boda & J. Gordon McConville (Downers Grove: InterVarsity Press, 2012): 99. von Rad identifies that this promissory type of covenant in Abraham is the first stage of priestly understanding of covenant concept (Gen 17:1-14) in the three-tier system what he calls: Abraham became a people, then Yahweh's new relationship with people through Sinai covenant is initiated, and then finally the possession of the land by the people has taken place.

to David that his dynasty would continue on the throne of Judah and that promise is a divine gift to David (2 Sam 7:1-17 and 1 Chr 17:1-15) without imposing any specific obligations. This is also called a grant type of covenant because of the reason that "the grant par excellence is an act of royal benevolence arising from the king's desire to reward his royal servant."[116] Weinfeld rightly remarked that:

> 2 Sam 7:18-29, with its notion of the Davidic covenant as humanity's character, provided for the future of the race under the leadership of Davidic house and thus foreshadowed the fulfillment of Abrahamic promises.[117]

3.7.3. The Mosaic Covenant

The covenant during Mosaic period is very crucial one since it is believed that through the Sinai covenant God entered into a special relationship with the people of Israel and also the people know Yahweh in a special way. Mosaic covenant is also understood in the context of commandments.[118] Two things can be stated on this point: first, Israel has encountered a unique experience with a holy God; second, the covenant or agreement however is made on the basis of Israel's total obedience and surrender to divine grace.[119]

3.7.4. The Deuteronomic Covenant

In Deuteronomy, not because of the merits of the people but because of Yahweh's grace God entered into a special relationship with the people of Israel. Its validity can be seen only only through

---

Jesurathnam, *Old Testament Theology: History, Issues, and Perspectives*, 220.

116 M. Wienfeld, *Deuteronomy and Deuteronomic school* (Oxford: Clarendon Press, 1972), 77.

117 Dumbrell, *Covenant and Creation*, 163.

118 Gerstenberger, "Covenant and Commandment," 38.

119 Walther Zimmerli, *Old Testament Theology in Outline* (Atlanta: John Knox Press, 1978), 53. See also Jathana, "The Covenant and Covenant Making in Pentateuch," *BTF*: 45-48.

people's total obedience to Yahweh (Deut 7:7-18). Deuteronomic covenant can be understood in the context of the land. It derives this land theology from the older covenant traditions of Abraham and David. von Rad points out that the Deuteronomy's concern for the land has to be seen in the total perspective of Israel's redemption.[120] Thus, the idea of covenant and the land theology are interrelated in Deuteronomy.

3.7.5. The New Covenant

New covenant denotes future relationship between God and his people following the collapse of the Mosaic covenant and Israel's loss of nationhood in 587 BCE. This new relationship is anticipated in other terms by Jeremiah and also by Ezekiel, Second Isaiah, and Malachi. According to Lundbom,

> The new covenant forms the centerpiece of a larger eschatological hope which includes a new act of salvation, a new Zion, and a new Davidic king.[121]

The belief in a new covenant existed among the Essenes of Qumran, but it was the Christian Church that laid real claim to Jeremiah's promise. In the NT the phrase *new covenant* appears in Luke 22:20, in Paul's Corinthian correspondence (1 Cor 11:25; 2 Cor 3:6), and in the Letter to the Hebrews (Heb 8:8,13; 9:15; *fresh covenant* in 12:24).[122]

---

120 Gerhard von Rad, *The Problem of Hexateuch and Other Essays* (Edinburgh: Oliver & Boyd, 1966), 95. On this point the views of Patrick D. Miller is worth considering. Miller argues that the land theology in Deuteronomy has to be seen in the context of God's gift to the people of Israel, the land. Israel's very existence as people and nation is in their possession of land which is a gift from Yahweh. Patrick D. Miller Jr., "The gift of God: The Deuteronomic Theology of the land," *Interpretation* 23 (1969): 451-465.

121 Jack R. Lundbom, "New Covenant," *ABD*, vol. 4, eds. David Noel Freedman, et al. (London: Doubleday, 1992): 1088.

122 Lundbom, "New Covenant," *ABD*: 1088.

3.7.5.1. OT

The expression *new covenant* appears only in the book of Jeremiah (31:31-34), but the concept is present in other Prophetic Books, such as Isaiah, Ezekiel, Hosea and Malachi. Isaiah anticipates the new covenant primarily through the Servant Songs (Is 42:1-9; 49:1-13; 50:4-11; 52:13-53:12). The Servant of Yahweh is the agent through whom God's covenant blessing will be extended to all people. God declares that this servant himself will be *a covenant for the people* (Is 42:6). The new covenant is also anticipated by Isaiah through the promise of the eternal covenant of peace (Is 54:10).[123] Like Jeremiah, Ezekiel emphasizes that the institution of the new covenant in the hearts of the people is possible only through the presence of God's Spirit in the people's hearts. Twice in the book of Ezekiel, God promises to give the people a new heart and to put his Spirit within them (Ezek 11:19; 36:26). Only under such conditions can the people now obey God's rules and commandments (Ezek 36:27).[124]

3.7.5.2. Literature of Judaism Including Qumran

In the Second Temple period the covenant idea is mainly characterized by an eschatological hope. National life has been reconstructed along the old lines, the Mosaic covenant is again central and the Law (*Torah*) occupies a position of supremacy. In Nehemiah 9-10 a *faith covenant* is made to walk according to Yahweh's Law given through Moses. Ezra prays that the people will thereby return to the *faithful heart* of Abraham (9:7–8). At the same time a new covenant is looked for in the future, at which time the Messianic Age will dawn. Among the Essenes at Qumran the new covenant finds fulfilment in a separated community who believes in the *last days*. The Essene covenant theology is

---

123 The Servant of Yahweh as described in Isaiah will inaugurate a new covenant that has the Davidic covenant as its basis, thus one that is linked to messianic hopes. This is an everlasting covenant associated with the person and work of the Servant of Yahweh, and will thus result in everlasting joy (Is 55:3; 61:8). Rata, "Covenant," 103-104.

124 Rata, "Covenant," 104.

contained in two sectarian documents of the Manual of Discipline (1QS), and the Damascus Document (CD). The new covenant idea undergoes no further development in Judaism.[125]

Conclusion

From the above discussions of covenant in the ancient and biblical world and its etymological and related significant concerns, the following conclusions can be drawn:

First, the concept of covenant is not determined by the term *bĕrît* itself because even where the term is not explicitly mentioned the spiritual promises of the covenant relationship with God are manifestly present. Rather it was determined by the basis of the relationship with God and the covenant-union between Yahweh and Israel.

Second, covenant is undoubtedly a major theological motif in the OT that has been always active between the Israelites and Yahweh, both individually and as a community. Israel is thus called the covenant community in covenant with God. As such the idea of covenant runs from OT through the NT.

Third, from the etymological study, *bĕrît* may be defined as *an agreement and relationship between Yahweh and the people, between human and human, and between human and other creations in which Yahweh is the initiator*. It is a living process in and through which God reveals God's will, which is a guiding principle for human being and his or her fellow-creations in order that they might live together harmoniously with peace and justice.

Fourth, as scholars have observed, the reason why the idea of covenant is similar in the AWA and ancient Israel is that there was a type of international treaty from the Hittite Empire at the approximate time of the beginning of the people of Israel. The primary purpose of the suzerainty treaty was to establish a firm relationship between the suzerain and his vassal. Thus, the tribes of Israel were bound together by a covenant based on religion and modelled after the suzerainty treaty by which the Hittite king bound his vassals to faithfulness and obedience to himself.

125 Lundbom, "New Covenant," *ABD*: 1090.

On the other hand, scholars criticize the analogy drawn between AWA treaties and OT covenant because the key theological concepts in the OT covenant texts emphasize the exclusive worship of Yahweh, the notion of Yahweh as a jealous God, the incomparability of Yahweh, etc. Thus, some scholars propose that the treaty texts must be rejected and the idea of covenant should be taken as a theological idea rather than social reality.

Fifth, Eichrodt notes that Jeremiah makes no explicit reference to the *bĕrît* during the first period of his activity, adding that things are different from the Josianic Reform onward. He does accord it more significance and yet uses it as one favourable method of conveying his prophetic message. He contrasts the old covenant with the new covenant of the age of salvation, in which God establishes a new and inward relationship with human by transforming their hearts.[126] This point is very significant in the interpretation of Jeremiah.

Sixth, as has already been indicated, there was no consensus among scholars regarding the meaning, definition and date of the word *bĕrît*. Among several scholars, Lothar Perlitt argued that Israel's covenant traditions are the product of a late period in its history and arose in response to various theological needs and crises. He proposed that for the eighth century prophets, covenant theology did not yet exist. His arguments may look controversial in some sense, but one can notice a shift and development in the understanding of the covenant through his work.

Finally, the study probably shows that the concept of covenant has been developed and changed from time to time. In other word, the concept of covenant has been changed according to the context and their needs. Previously the old covenant concept was exclusively for Israel. But later on, we find the inclusive nature of the covenant.

126 Eichrodt, *Theology of the Old Testament I*, 59.

Chapter 4

Exegetical Analysis of Covenant Motif in Relation to New Covenant in Jeremiah

Introduction

The researcher has dealt with the etymology and concept of covenant in the AWA and Biblical world in the preceding chapter. It has been observed that covenant is an agreement and relationship that has been active between Yahweh and Israel, as a community and individual. It was likely that the idea of the covenant in the AWA has close affinity with the covenant idea in the OT. Further, Jeremiah used various covenant traditions of both obligatory and promissory covenant. Therefore, it gave a clue that the book of Jeremiah had a deep interest in the covenant between Yahweh and Israel.

A number of questions arise out of the concern of Jeremiah with the covenant idea. However, the guiding questions for our exegetical task are: What was Jeremiah's actual thinking of the covenant? What has happened and why it is even necessary to speak about new covenant? What are the covenantal principles

Jeremiah taught to the community of Judah? How Jeremiah's views on the ethics of the covenant are related to such a pattern or can they be explained on some other basis? Why Jeremiah shifted his thinking from the idea of covenant to the new covenant? In order to answer the above questions, the following texts are selected for analysis.

4.1. Text,[127] Translation and its Philological Analysis

4.2. Jeremiah 7:1-15: Covenantal Principles

4.2.1. Translation

v. 1. [a]The word that came to Jeremiah from the Lord.

v. 2. Stand in the gate of the Lord's house, and proclaim there this word, and say, Hear the word of the Lord, all you people of Judah, you that enter these gates to worship the Lord.[a]

v. 3. Thus says the Lord of hosts, the God of Israel: Amend your ways and your doings, and [a]let me dwell with you[a] in this place.

v. 4. Do not trust in these deceptive[a] words: "This is the temple of the Lord, the temple of the Lord, these are[b] the temple of the Lord."

v. 5. For if you truly amend your ways and your doings, if you truly act justly one with another,

v. 6. If you do not oppress the alien, the orphan, and the widow, or [b]shed innocent blood in this place[b], and if you do not go after other gods to your own hurt

v. 7. Then I will dwell with you in this place, in the land that I gave of old to your ancestors forever and ever.

v. 8. Here you are, trusting in deceptive words to no avail.

127 The Hebrew Text followed for our English translation is K. Ellinger and W. Rudolph (eds.) *Biblia Hebraica Stuttgartensia* 4th edition (Stuttgart: Deutsche Bibelgesellschaft, 1990).

v. 9. Will you steal, murder, commit adultery, swear falsely, make offerings to Baal, and go after other gods that you have not known,

v. 10. And then come and stand before me in this house, which is called by my name, and say, "We are safe!"—only to go on doing all these abominations?

v. 11. Has his[a] house, which is called by my name, become a den of robbers in your sight? You know, I too am watching, says the Lord.

v. 12. Go now to my place that was in Shiloh, where I made my name dwell at first, and see what I did to it for the wickedness of my people Israel.

v. 13. And now, because you have done all these things, says the Lord, and when I spoke to you persistently, you did not listen, and when I called you, you did not answer,

v. 14. Therefore I will do to the house that is called by my name, in which you trust, and to the place that I gave to you and to your ancestors, just what I did to Shiloh.

v. 15. And I will cast you out of my sight, just as I cast out all your kinsfolk, all the offspring of Ephraim.

4.2.2. Textual Notes

Words of vv. 1-2[a-a] are lacking in LXX. Volz and Rudolph accept them, but Janzen gives careful argumentation in favor of rejecting them.[128] Of v. 3[a-a], MT וַאֲשַׁכְּנָה אֶתְכֶם (pi'el verb) *so that I may let you dwell* understands *this place* as referring to the land. But, the temple is here the center of interest. The *place* that Yahweh chooses is regularly the temple.[129] In v. 4[a] LXX adds ὅτι τὸ

128 William L. Holladay, *Jeremiah 1: A Commentary on the Book of Prophet Jeremiah Chapters 1-25* (Philadelphia: Fortress Press, 1986), 235.

129 John Bright, *Jeremiah: A New Translation with Introduction and Commentary, AB* (New York: Double Day Company, 1965), 55.

παράπαν οὐκ ὠφελήσουσιν ὑμᾶς, but are missing in MT and the other Versions. In v. 4[b] we find המה, *these*, BHS suggests it is an abbreviation, הם (for המקום) and ה (for הזה), *this place* (v. 3).[130] Of v. 6[b-b] Bright is of the view that the negative in this clause is אל, which must be translated as a prohibition, *and do not shed innocent blood in this place*.[131] Of v. 11[a-a] LXX reads ὁ οἶκός μου *my house*: the possessive μου seems to be dittographic from *my name* five words later.[132]

4.2.3. Form, Structure and Setting

According to Brueggemann, the unit presents Jeremiah's so-called *temple sermon*, perhaps the clearest and most formidable statement of the basic themes of the Jeremiah tradition.[133] The chapter is largely in prose, except possibly for vv. 15-16, and it has been argued that the styles is *Deuteronomic* and therefore reflects the Deuteronomic method of thinking.[134] However, Holladay denies a widely held belief that Jer 7:1-15 is the work of a Deuteronomistic redactor.[135] Thompson argues, *there is no necessity to doubt that the passage reflects Jeremiah's actual thinking*.[136]

According to Holladay, the genre is parenesis (that is, moral exhortation) based upon covenant formulations, so that perhaps *covenant speech* is the most accurate term. The covenant mediator reminds the hearers of their covenant obligations and urges them

130 Peter C. Craigie, *Jeremiah 1-25: WBC*, vol. 26 (Dallas: Word Incorporated, 2002), 116.

131 Bright, *Jeremiah, AB*, 56.

132 Holladay, *Jeremiah 1*, 236.

133 Brueggemann, *A Commentary on Jeremiah: Exile and Homecoming,* 77.

134 E. W. Nicholson regards only vv. 15-16 as Jeremiah's. The whole section is a Deuteronomic composition. If there is any genuine Jeremianic saying behind the utterance it has been so recast the words of Jeremiah have disappeared. E.W. Nicholson, *Jeremiah 1-25: Cambridge Bible Commentary on the New English Bible* (Cambridge University Press: Cambridge, 1973), 108f.

135 Holladay, *Jeremiah 1*, 240.

136 Thompson, *The Book of Jeremiah, NICOT*, 61.

to adhere to that which they have promised.[137] The structure of the sermon follows a particular pattern: a) the proclamation of Yahweh's word and law (vv. 1-7); b) the description of the nation's apostasy (vv. 8-12); the announcement of judgment (vv. 13-15).[138] This section appears to be a longer form of the sermon referred to in Jer 26:1-6. The date of the passage, therefore, in its original proclamation, would be approximately 609-608 BCE, early in king Jehoiakim's reign.[139]

4.2.4. Exegetical Comments and Interpretation in Relation to New Covenant Motif

The temple sermon claims that it is the responsibility of all the people of Judah to execute justice. Jeremiah demands that those coming to the temple *amend your ways and your doings* (v. 5). Among Jeremiah's specific admonitions is a call to "act justly one with another...not oppress the alien, the orphan, and the widow, or shed innocent blood" (vv. 5-6). These admonitions, addressed to *all you people of Judah* (v. 4), again echo the ways that Judah's kings were to be responsible for justice.[140] According to Patrick D. Miller, "Fair and just dealings; protection and care of the innocent and weak members of the society; and unqualified devotion and loyalty to the Lord are required."[141] Thus the Decalogue mentioned are cardinal principles that a covenant community is expected to follow for the well-being of the entire society.

What the prophet does here is to present various covenant principles as was done in the case of other prophets like Isa 1:16-17; Ezek 45:9; Mic 6:8; Zech 7:8-10. As a result of these words the prophet expects the people to live a desired life for Yahweh as

137 Holladay, *Jeremiah 1*, 239.

138 Thompson, *The Book of Jeremiah*, *NICOT,* 274.

139 Craigie, *Jeremiah 1-25*, *WBC,* 119.

140 John M. Bracke, "Justice in the Book of Jeremiah," *Word and World* 22/4 (Fall 2002): 391.

141 Miller, "The Book of Jeremiah," *NIB*: 636.

a covenant community.[142] Jeremiah wanted his contemporaries to see that Yahweh is against all individual promise of covenant if it is not in agreement with the demands of social justice. Jeremiah wanted the people to realize that the covenant demands of Yahweh are far more superior and vital than any individual promises that God had made in the past. Any individualism cannot stand against God's wider plan.[143] Jesurathnam rightly remarked:[144]

> Israel as the covenant community is expected to fulfil certain obligations in their true devotion to Yahweh. In the temple sermon in Jer 7:1-15, Jeremiah reminds the already stated fundamental covenantal principles as we know from the other prophets that people should follow. So, that the revival or even the very survival of Judah is based on the observance of these fundamental guidelines. The truth is very plainly stated in the sense that even the well established and fundamental tradition of people's salvation in the institute of the Jerusalem temple will not save them without them following the covenantal principles of justice and righteousness.

4.3. Jeremiah 7:21-26: Covenantal Obedience not Sacrifice

4.3.1. Translation

v. 21. Thus says the Lord of hosts, the God of Israel: Put your burnt offerings with your other sacrifices[a], and eat the flesh.

---

142 K. Jesurathnam, "Transforming Praxis: God, Community, Church-Reading Jeremiah 7:1-15 (Temple Sermon with Special Focus on Dalit Christian Response)," *Transforming Praxis: God, Community and Church, Essays in Honour of Dr. I. John Mohan Razu*, ed. C.I. David Joy (Bangalore: UTC, 2008), 122-123.

143 Jesurathnam, "Transforming Praxis: God, Community, Church-Reading Jeremiah 7:1-15: 120.

144 Jesurathnam, "Transforming Praxis: God, Community, Church-Reading Jeremiah 7:1-15: 112.

v. 22. For in the day that I brought your ancestors out of the land of Egypt, I did not speak to them or command them concerning burnt offerings and sacrifices.

v. 23. But this command I gave them, "Obey[a] my voice, and I will be your God, and you shall be my people; and walk only in the way that I command you, so that it may be well with you."

v. 24. Yet they did not obey or incline their ear, but, in the stubbornness of their evil will, they walked in their own counsels, and went backward rather than forward.

v. 25. From the day that your ancestors came out of the land of Egypt until this day, I have persistently sent to you all my servants the prophets to them, day after day;

v. 26. Yet they did not listen to me, or pay attention, but they stiffened their necks. They did worse than their ancestors did.

4.3.2. Textual Notes

In v. 21[a] *other* is added to bring out the sense. For Bright, the point seems to be that God does not care which way sacrifice is performed. The force of this passage is much disputed. It is unlikely that it is to be taken either as a categorical rejection of the sacrificial system as such. The point lies in the balance between the two.[145] Of v. 23[a], the Hebrew for *obey* is שִׁמְעוּ בְ, *ear into*. The preposition may be regarded as emphasizing the personal commitment of the subject of the object. God required of Israel deep personal commitment to God's voice.[146]

4.3.3. Form, Structure and Setting

Verse 21 begins a new unit.[147] The unit is full of Deuteronomistic phrases and concepts such as obedience, sacrifice etc. There is

145 Bright, *Jeremiah, AB,* 56-57.

146 Thompson, *The Book of Jeremiah, NICOT,* 288.

147 Holladay, *Jeremiah 1*, 259.

disagreement among commentators about how the unit should be divided: vv. 21-26 (Bright),[148] 21-28 (Thompson,[149] Holladay[150]), 21-29 (Miller[151]). Carroll is of the opinion that if vv. 21-26 are the divine address to the nation and vv. 27-28 an address to the speaker, it is better to treat them separately in order to emphasize the different features of each speech.[152] While vv. 16-20 are an address in the second-person singular in Jeremiah, vv. 21 and 22 shift to the plural to address the people. Vv. 21-23 offer a parody of priestly *torah* that is cultic instructions in the imperative plural, followed by an evaluative concluding statement introduced by כִּי (v. 22). The command is followed in v. 23 by the covenant formula, *I will be your God, and you shall be my people*. Vv. 24-26 offer an accusation report, a statement by Yahweh of the disobedience of the covenant people in both past and present.[153]

4.3.4. Exegetical Comments and Interpretation in Relation to New Covenant Motif

These verses expand on the contrast already made in Jer 7:3-4 between covenantal obedience and manipulation in liturgy. The critique of Israel's worship in the face of its disobedience continues in these verses. The assault on the ideological claims and practices of the Jerusalem establishment is unqualified and relentless. It is asserted that God of Israel has never been interested in sacrificial liturgy (vv. 21-22). Brueggemann opines that 'the practice of such sacrifice tends to serve and legitimate vested social interest, and thus takes aim against covenantal obedience.'[154] What is commanded and required is listening (v. 23). Listening is the

148 Bright, *Jeremiah, AB,* 58.

149 Thompson, *The Book of Jeremiah, NICOT,* 286.

150 Holladay, *Jeremiah 1*, 259.

151 Miller, "The Book of Jeremiah: Introduction, Commentary, and Reflections," *NIB*: 639.

152 Robert P. Carroll, *Jeremiah: A Commentary* (Philadelphia: Westminster Press, 1986), 214.

153 Holladay, *Jeremiah 1*, 259.

154 Brueggemann, *A Commentary on Jeremiah: Exile and Homecoming,* 83.

primal act of covenantal responsiveness (Deut 6:4). The phrase *If you listen to my voice* and its continuation *and keep my covenant* is followed by God's promise: *then you shall be my possessions out of all peoples*. V. 23 now says that when God brought Israel's fathers out of Egypt he said to them: *Listen to my voice, then I will be your God and you shall be my people*. V. 23 reflects the narrative of the Exodus.

The texts in Ex 19 and Jer 7 are therefore related as the covenant formula is followed by the demand that the people listen to God's voice. But the difference between the two texts is: First, in Jeremiah 7 the bilateral covenant formula is used, whereas in Ex 19 we find only the incomplete formula. Second, in the context of Jeremiah 7 the word *bĕrît* is missing, whereas in Ex 19 it plays a central part.[155] The fundamental claim of the passage is once again an insistence that the covenantal relationship is about obedience.[156] God's essential demands did not concern ritual matters, but the keeping of the covenant stipulations.

4.4. Jeremiah 11:1-14: Covenant Foundation and Demands

4.4.1. Translation

v. 1. The word that came to Jeremiah from the LORD:

v. 2. Hear[a] the words of this covenant[b], and speak[c] to the people of Judah and the inhabitants of Jerusalem.

v. 3. You shall say to them, thus says the Lord, the God of Israel: Cursed be anyone who does not heed the words of this covenant,

v. 4. which I commanded your ancestors when I brought them out of the land of Egypt, from the iron-smelter, saying, Listen to my voice, and do them according to

155 Rolf Rendtorff, *The Covenant Formula: An Exegetical and Theological Investigation* (Edinburg: T&T Clark, 1998), 31-32.

156 Miller, "The Book of Jeremiah: Introduction, Commentary, and Reflections," *NIB:* 639.

all that I command you. So shall you be my people, and I will be your God,

v. 5. that I may perform the oath that I swore to your ancestors, to give them a land flowing with milk and honey, as at this day. Then I answered, "So be it, Lord."

v. 6. And the Lord said to me: Proclaim all these words in the cities of Judah, and in the streets of Jerusalem: Hear the words of this covenant and do them.

v. 7. [a]For I solemnly warned your ancestors when I brought them up out of the land of Egypt, warning them persistently, even to this day, saying, Obey my voice.

v. 8. Yet they did not obey or incline their ear, but everyone walked in the stubbornness of an evil will. So I brought upon them all the words of this covenant, which I commanded[a] them to do, but they did not.

v. 9. And the Lord said to me: Conspiracy exists among the people of Judah and the inhabitants of Jerusalem.

v. 10. They have turned back to the iniquities of their ancestors of old, who refused to heed my words; they have gone after other gods to serve them; the house of Israel and the house of Judah have broken the covenant that I made with their ancestors.

v. 11. Therefore, thus says the Lord, assuredly I am going to bring disaster upon them that they cannot escape; though they cry out to me, I will not listen to them.

v. 12. Then the cities of Judah and the inhabitants of Jerusalem will go and cry out to the gods to whom they make offerings, but they will never save them in the time of their trouble.

v. 13. For your gods have become as many as your towns, O Judah; and as many as the streets of Jerusalem are the altars to shame you have set up, altars to make offerings to Baal.

v. 14. As for you, do not pray for this people, or lift up a cry or prayer on their behalf, for I will not listen when they call to me in the time of their trouble.

4.4.2. Textual Notes

V. 2/3[a-a] may be later addition. Holladay argues that MT of this section of v. 2 is impossible. V. 3 begins with a singular verb *and you shall say*. In LXX the reference shifts from imperative plural in the first verb of v. 2 to second singular in the second verb.[157] Of v. 2[b], Rudolph and Weiser assume that the ברית which is in view is the Sinai covenant rather than Deuteronomy. Thiel holds that it does not have the concreteness to represent the prophet Jeremiah as a Deuteronomic preacher.[158] In v. 2[c] LXX reads καὶ λαλήσεις (*and speak*) compared with Syriac.[159] Holladay argues that v. 7/8[a-a] is omitted from LXX and some consider this expansionistic. LXX represents a more authentic text tradition, while MT has expanded the text secondarily.[160]

4.4.3. Form, Structure and Setting

According to Holladay vv. 1-14, like Jer 7:1-12, are a covenant speech offered by Jeremiah, who functions as a covenant mediator.[161] Carroll too is of the view that this lengthy section presents Jeremiah as a preacher of the covenant.[162] Many scholars thought this chapter was the work of Deuteronomic editors around 550 BCE who may have used some of Jeremiah's words or composed them in the spirit of Jeremiah.[163] John Bright, on the other hand, opines *there is no reason to doubt that it reflects*

157 Holladay, *Jeremiah 1*, 346.

158 William McKane, *A Critical and Exegetical Commentary on Jeremiah* (Edinburgh: T&T Clark International, 1986), 244.

159 Craigie, *Jeremiah 1-25, WBC*, 167.

160 Holladay, *Jeremiah 1*, 346.

161 Holladay, *Jeremiah 1*, 352.

162 Carroll, *Jeremiah*, 267.

163 Huey, *Jeremiah, Lamentations, NAC*, 132.

Jeremiah's actual sentiments and activity.[164] In this sermon the catastrophe has already happened, so it is too late to warn the community. It is preached to those living after the disaster and is intended to warn them about the consequences of disobedience. Nicholson rightly remarks, 'it represents the actualization for a later generation of the Word of Yahweh spoken by the prophet Jeremiah to an earlier generation.'[165]

Carroll proposes that the unit may be divided into a number of sub-sections: vv. 1-5, 6-8, 9-13 with 14 as a redactional addition.[166] For Kizzhakeyil, the sequence of the chapter offers an outline of the old covenant formulary: covenant foundation (vv. 1-5); (ancient) covenant violation (vv. 6-8); (contemporary) covenant violation (vv. 9-13); harsh judgment and end of the covenant relationship (vv. 14-17).[167] Many commentators classify this passage as exilic or post-exilic.[168] For Bright, the passage seems in the main to relate to Jehoiakim's reign and it is of exilic date.[169]

4.4.4. Exegetical Comments and Interpretation in Relation to New Covenant Motif

This passage deals with the issues related to the demands of the covenant. Rolf Rendtorff is of the view that the word *bĕrît* is at the centre in Jer 11. Jeremiah is charged to preach about the covenant.[170] For Thompson, the main thrush of this section is to urge obedience to *this covenant* and then to castigate the people

---

164 Bright, *Jeremiah, AB*, 89.

165 E. W. Nicholson, *Preaching to the Exiles: A Study of the Prose Tradition in the Book of Jeremiah* (Basil: Blackwell, 1970), 67.

166 Nicholson, *Jeremiah 1-25*, 108.

167 Sebastian Kizhakkeyil, *Jeremiah: An Exegetical Commentary* (Bangalore: ATC, 2006), 72.

168 John Bright, *A History of Israel*, 3rd ed. (Philadelphia: Westminster, 1981), 328-330.

169 Bright, *Jeremiah, AB*, 89.

170 Rendtorff, *The Covenant Formula*, 32.

for their breach of it.[171] The expression *this covenant* may refer to the covenant enacted by Josiah or a more general reference to the covenant associated with Sinai. However, according to Carroll, the distinction between the two senses of covenant should not be overstressed.[172]

In this passage, the prophet wants to affirm the demands of the Sinai covenant as against the people who cherish royal covenant upheld by the leaders in Jerusalem.[173] For Brueggemann, vv. 1-5 present three important themes of the tradition. First, Judah and Jerusalem must listen. This listening is to be done in terms of being obedient to the covenant. Second, through listening and being obedient to the covenant Judah and Yahweh belong to one another affirmed by means of the covenant formula. Third, as a sign of God's covenant with the people the gift of land is linked directly to the obedience of the people to Yahweh's covenant. All three elements indicate that Jeremiah is commissioned by Yahweh to express and summon Israel to the most demanding and elemental claims of covenant faith.[174]

Jeremiah tells the people that they have broken the covenant of Yahweh.[175] As Judah revolts against the covenant (vv. 9-13), God will refuse to listen to them, realizing that other gods cannot help them.[176] The text takes up the old conventional language of covenant and applies it to Jeremiah's contemporaries. Covenant violation leads to historical destruction. For this community defined in covenantal ways, disobedience to covenant can only

171 Thompson, *The Book of Jeremiah*, *NICOT*, 61.

172 Carroll, *From Chaos to Covenant,* 96-97. See Thompson, *The Book of Jeremiah*, *NICOT*, 61. Similarly, Bright prudently warned against making too sharp a distinction between these two covenants. Bright, *Jeremiah, AB*, 89.

173 Jesurathnam, *Exploring Dalit Liberative Hermeneutic in India & the World*, 155.

174 Brueggemann, *A Commentary on Jeremiah: Exile and Homecoming,* 109-111.

175 Kizhakkeyil, *Jeremiah: An Exegetical Commentary*, 73.

176 Kizhakkeyil, *Jeremiah: An Exegetical Commentary*, 73.

lead to death. If God destroys covenant relationship with Judah everything in her live is nullified and she will lose all her identity among the world nations.[177]

4.5. Jeremiah 24:4-7: Covenant of Life and Blessing, Death and Curse

4.5.1. Translation

v. 4. Then the word of the Lord came to me

v. 5. [a]Thus says the Lord, the God of Israel[a]: Like these good figs, so I will regard as good the exiles from Judah, whom I have sent away from this place to the land of the Chaldeans.

v. 6. I will set my eyes[a] upon them for good, and I will bring them back to this land. I will build them up, and not tear them down; I will plant them, and not pluck them up.

v. 7. I will give them a heart to know that I am the Lord; and they shall be my people and I will be their God, for they shall return to me with their whole heart.

4.5.2. Textual Notes

Regarding v. 5[a-a] BHS labels this phrase as an addition. Rudolph also deletes as the formal messenger speech introduction does not fit the private nature of the communication given to Jeremiah by Yahweh.[178] Of v. 6[a] a few manuscripts, LXX, and Vulgate have the plural *eyes*.[179]

4.5.3. Form, Structure and Setting

The chapter has the form of a prophetic vision that captures the theme of this section of the book about life and blessing, death

177 Brueggemann, *A Commentary on Jeremiah: Exile and Homecoming,* 112.

178 Carroll, *Jeremiah*, 481.

179 Holladay, *Jeremiah 1*, 654.

and curse.[180] According to W. Zimmerli, there are three types of visions in Jeremiah: first, the two visions of 1:11-15; secondly, the unit 4:23-26 and finally, chapter 24, which in its present form is Deuteronomistic.[181] Form-critically considered, Jer 24 consists of an elaborately constructed account of a vision, containing within itself elements of the Deuteronomistic preaching of alternatives. S. Hermann and Thiel have argued that the vocabulary and the theological outlook of Jer 24 are the work of Deuteronomistic redaction because the introduction to Jer 24 explicitly names Yahweh as the author of the vision, and in this respect it is closer to the four visions in Amos 7:1-8; 8:1-2 than Jer 1:1-15.[182] Therefore, it seems to be Deuteronomistic redaction. The oracle falls into two nearly balanced halves, the good figs being identified in the first half with exiles and the bad figs in the second half with Zedekiah and the ones remaining in the land. The historical context is indicated by the references to the exile of Jeconiah-Jehoiachin and the reign of Zedekiah. That setting gives a date for the vision between 597 and 587 BCE.[183]

4.5.4. Exegetical Comments and Interpretation in Relation to New Covenant Motif

In Jer 24:4-7 we find the covenant formula in a wholly new context. These are the first years of the exile, and Jeremiah sees in a vision two baskets of figs, some very good and some very bad. The good figs are identified with the Judeans in exile. These exiles are now presented as the object and recipient of God's gracious intervention. God *set my eyes* upon them for good (v. 6). God resolves to return them from exile and to permit them to resume

---

180 John M. Bracke, *Jeremiah 1-29, Westminster Bible Companion* (Westminster: John Knox Press, 2000), 195.

181 Thomas Vallianippuram, *Jeremiah: A Prophet of the Modern World* (Bangalore: Dharmaram Publications, 2012), 24.

182 Walther Zimmerli, "Visionary Experience in Jeremiah," *Israel's Prophetic Tradition: Essays in Honour of Peter R. Ackroyd*, eds. R. Coggins et al. (Cambridge: University Press, 1982), 105.

183 Craigie, *Jeremiah 1-25, WBC*, 357.

life in the land. In v. 6 the narrative utilizes the powerful verbs of Jer 1:10. According to Bruegemann, now the positive verbs *plant* and *build* are operative. Indeed, *tearing down and plucking up* have already happened, and now God restores.[184]

This proclamation reaches its climax in v. 7. Rendtorff is of the view that the covenant formula points to the future. What is new here is that the salvific future still impending in which Israel will then turn back to God with its whole and new heart. God will make a new beginning, which will be subject to the covenant formula, as the summary expression of God's relationship to the people. The new heart will bring about knowledge.[185] Brueggemann opines,[186]

> The purpose of the new heart for Israel is for the sake of a restored covenant with Yahweh. The covenant formula indicates that Israel's autonomy has now been happily displaced by an embrace of covenant.

4.6. Jeremiah 32:36-41: Everlasting Covenant

4.6.1. Translation

> v. 36. Now therefore[a] thus says the Lord, the God of Israel, concerning this city of which [b]you say[b], "It is being given into the hand of the king of Babylon by the sword, by famine, and by pestilence."
>
> v. 37. See, I am going to gather them from all the lands to which I drove them in my anger and my wrath and in great indignation; I will bring them back to this place, and I will settle them in safety.
>
> v. 38. They shall be my people, and I will be their God.

184 Brueggemann, *A Commentary on Jeremiah: Exile and Homecoming,* 218.

185 Rendtorff, *The Covenant Formula*, 33.

186 Brueggemann, *A Commentary on Jeremiah: Exile and Homecoming,* 218.

v. 39. I will give them one heart and [a]one way[a], that they may fear me for all time, for their own good and the good of their children after them.

v. 40. I will make an everlasting covenant with them, that I will not turn away[a] from after them from doing good to them; and I will put the fear of me in their hearts, so that they may not turn from me.

v. 41. [a]I will rejoice[a] in doing good to them, and I will plant them in this land in faithfulness, with all my heart and all my soul.

4.6.2. Textual Notes

V. 36[a] is omitted in LXX and Syriac, MT adds clarification. Of v. 36[b], LXX has καὶ ἐν ἀποστολῇ, *and by banishment*, for MT's ובדבר, *by pestilence* compare with v. 24, where LXX lacks the third part of the stereotyped expression.[187] With regard to v. 39[a-a], it literally means *one heart and one way* (cf. Ezek 11:19). But LXX reverses the order, ὁδὸν ἑτέραν καὶ καρδίαν ἑτέραν, *another way and another heart*. Perhaps MT should be preferred as the more difficult reading.[188] LXX reads v. 40[a] ἀποστρέψω *to turn away, mislead* and in v. 41[a-a], LXX has καὶ ἐπισκέψομαι ... αὐτούς, and *I will visit them*, a more common expression, consistent with the following clause.[189]

4.6.3. Form, Structure and Setting

According to Dalit Rom-Shiloni, vv. 36-41 in Jer 32 (and in fact most of vv. 16-44) were considered Deuteronomistic redaction by Duhm and subsequently by many other scholars.[190] Hence, there

187 Gerald L. Keown, *Jeremiah 26-52: WBC*, vol. 27 (Dallas: Word Incorporated, 2002), 144.

188 Bright, *Jeremiah*, *AB*, 295.

189 Keown, *Jeremiah 26-52, WBC*, 144.

190 Dalit Rom-Shiloni, "The Prophecy for "Everlasting Covenant" (Jeremiah XXXII 36-41): An Exilic Addition or A Deuteronomistic Redactions?" *VT* LIII/2 (2003): 202.

is nothing new in arguing that this prophecy is non-Jeremian. He states that:[191]

> The prophecy of the *everlasting covenant* is undoubtedly of exilic origin. It adduces literal connections to Jeremiah's prophecies, and even imitates the rhetorical style of the prophet. Nevertheless, the prophecy differs considerably from the prophet's own words. The author adapts previous prophecies and reinterprets them to suit his own time-the Babylonian Exile.

Contrary to the general agreement, Bright suggested vv. 36-44 to be authentic oracle in reply to vv. 24-27.[192] Holladay considers vv. 36, 37 and 41 as authentic and leaves vv. 38-40 as later insertion.[193]

Form-critical considerations point out the self-contained status of vv. 36-41. Divided into two major parts: quotation (v. 36) and prophetic refutation (vv. 37-41), the prophetic unit is structured according to the form-pattern of the *disputation-speech.* This prophetical *genre* was identified by Gunkel and Westermann. Rom-Shiloni suggests that vv. 36-41 should be considered as another, yet unique, disputation-speech.[194] The literary history of this chapter was reconstructed in several different ways, pointing out the two main strata of the book and several additional comments.[195]

---

191 Rom-Shiloni, "The Prophecy for "Everlasting Covenant" (Jeremiah XXXII 36-41): An Exilic Addition or A Deuteronomistic Redactions?" *VT*: 222.

192 Bright, *Jeremiah, AB*, 289-292.

193 William L. Holladay, *Jeremiah 2: A Commentary on the Book of the Prophet Jeremiah Chapters 26-52* (Philadelphia: Fortress Press, 1990), 208.

194 Rom-Shiloni, "The Prophecy for "Everlasting Covenant" (Jeremiah XXXII 36-41): An Exilic Addition or A Deuteronomistic Redactions?" *VT*: 203.

195 Different perspectives and arguments are suggested in the commentaries, cf. Bright, *Jeremiah, AB*, 297-98; Carroll, *Jeremiah*, 627-632; Holladay, *Jeremiah 2*, 206-212; and M. Weinfeld, "Jeremiah and the Spiritual Metamorphosis in Israel," *ZAW* 88 (1976), 30-48.

4.6.4. Exegetical Comments and Interpretation in Relation to New Covenant Motif

According to Brueggemann, the following statements can be observed from vv. 36-41:[196] One, the covenantal formula, *they shall be my people, and I will be their God* (v. 38) asserts utter solidarity between God and Israel, a solidarity sharply disrupted by the Exile, but now fully restored. Two, a gift of a new heart, a new disposition toward Yahweh which permits full trust in God, which makes trustful obedience joyous (v. 39; cf. Ezek 11:19-20; 36:26-27). Three, an assertion of an *everlasting covenant*, one not to be disrupted or violated as exile disrupted and violated the old covenant.[197] Thus, it is precisely the exilic situation of radical discontinuity that evokes and permits such a full statement of confidence and of continuity (v. 40). Four, the promise that God will act in complete fidelity (אֱמֶת) to do good and to plant Israel in the land which had seemed forfeited (v. 41).

According to Rendtorff, the covenant formula is once again at the centre in this section. God will gather those who have been scattered, and bring them back to Jerusalem. Here this is summed up in v. 38. Again the heart plays a decisive role (vv. 39, 40b), and the *eternal covenant* which God is going to make with the people (v. 40a) is described in unequivocally plain terms as a covenant of grace, from which God will not depart.[198]

Conclusion

From the above discussion, we can summarize the findings of the study of the selected texts with the following points:

First, the covenantal principles Jeremiah taught to the community of Judah include the practice of justice and

---

196 Brueggemann, *A Commentary on Jeremiah: Exile and Homecoming,* 308-309.

197 The עוֹלָם בְּרִית emerges as especially important in the Exile when the covenant of Moses seemed to have been abrogated. See Delbert R. Hillers, *Covenant: The History of a Biblical Idea* (Baltimore: John Hopkins University Press, 1969), 98-119.

198 Rendtorff, *The Covenant Formula*, 34-35.

righteousness, obedience, non-oppression of alien, orphan or widow, the refusal to shed innocent blood and the avoidance of following other gods (Jer 7:5-6) that are found in the Decalogue.[199] Failure to execute the covenant principles did not merely jeopardize the survival of one king. Rather, Judah's very survival depends upon the execution of justice and righteousness by all the people.

Second, within the book of Jeremiah, we find a significant shift in the use and function of the covenant formula. In the temple sermon (Jer 7:1-15), there is no particular reference to the term covenant. But, the sermon points to Jeremiah's teaching of covenantalism. He reminds the fundamental covenant principles and urged them to fulfil all the demands.

Third, in Jer 7:21-26 the formula is related to the deliverance from Egypt and the demands that God had made with the Israelite that the people should listen to his voice. The formula suggests a particular function in the prophetic judgment sayings, because in the prophet's view Israel has not obeyed God's voice.

Fourth, the pericope in Jer 11:1-14 contains the covenant theology in summary form.[200] It probably reminds us that the covenant is not simply an abstract metaphor for speaking about relationship with God. It is the effecting of a relationship out of particular historical events: the Lord's deliverance of Israelite slaves from Egypt and the promise of a place for living that God made to their ancestors. These two dimensions of God's beneficent and redemptive care of a community are what evokes the covenantal relationship.[201] Covenant is thus the community's experience of having been redeemed and the possibilities of life that God promises. But, it is not finally a covenantal relationship until the community takes on its responsibility to the redeeming and promising God.

---

199 Jesurathnam, *Exploring Dalit Liberative Hermeneutics in India & the World*, 99.

200 Kizhakkeyil, *Jeremiah: An Exegetical Commentary*, 72.

201 Miller, "The Book of Jeremiah," *NIB:* 671.

Fifth, Jeremiah 24 marks the turning point. Obedience to the covenant stipulations brought blessing, breach of covenant brought a curse. God's judgment has descended upon Israel, and a dividing line is drawn between those who have been taken into Babylonian captivity and those who have remained behind in the land. The first group is now the bearer of the promise, and the covenant formula becomes a central saying of assurance. Hence, the covenant formula points to the future.

Sixth, Jer 32:36-41 introduces the everlasting covenant. This passage might have been originated from an exilic period. Therefore, it is different from the covenant formula mentioned above. Here the formula points to the promise of single heart and single nature. It was very similar to the promise in the new covenant. But the attribute עוֹלָם in this prophecy, meaning everlasting time ahead projects the future, and does not mention either past commitments or prior sin of the people. The everlasting covenant is to take effect on the exilic community after its return to the land. Whereas, the description of *the new covenant* does not contain a hint of the circumstances of exile and return.[202]

Finally, it can be maintained that the old covenant has its own limitations due to the changing circumstances and situations. Therefore, Jeremiah shifted his thinking of the old covenant to the new covenant that God has promised a new covenant, not like the previous covenant which will be dealt with in the next chapter.

---

202 Rom-Shiloni, "The Prophecy for "Everlasting Covenant" (Jeremiah XXXII 36-41): An Exilic Addition or A Deuteronomistic Redactions?" *VT:* 218.

Chapter 5

Exegetical Analysis of New Covenant in Jeremiah 31:31-34

Introduction

The preceding chapter gave a clear picture of the covenant idea of Jeremiah with a particular focus on various covenantal formula used by Jeremiah. The exegetical analysis of the texts shows that there is a significant shift in the use and function of covenant formula. It also attempts to relate the covenant concept of Jeremiah with the new covenant. Jeremiah urged the people to fulfil the covenantal demands of justice and righteousness, obedience and non-oppression of alien, orphan or widow.

In this chapter, the researcher deals with the selected text Jeremiah 31:31-34 by applying literary-critical method and other relevant methods when needed. In order to bring out the motif of the new covenant, some questions will be examined. Why Jeremiah shifted his thinking from the idea of covenant to the New Covenant? In what sense is the new covenant new? With whom is the new covenant made? What constitutes the continuity and the discontinuity of the new covenant? What is the place of *law* in the new covenant framework? What are the ethical teachings of the new covenant?

5.1. Translation

> v. 31. Behold the days are coming, says the Lord, when I will make a new covenant with the house of Israel [a]and the house of Judah[a].
>
> v. 32. It will not be like the covenant that I made with their ancestors when I took them by the hand to bring them out of the land of Egypt—a covenant that they[a] broke[b], though I[c] was their husband[d], says the Lord.
>
> v. 33. But, this is the covenant that I will make with the house of Israel after those days, says the Lord: I will put my law within them, and I will write it on their hearts; and I will be their God, and they shall be my people.
>
> v. 34. No longer shall they teach one another, or say to each other, "Know the Lord," for they shall all know me, from the least of them to the greatest, says the Lord; for I will forgive their iniquity, and remember their sin no more.

5.1.1. Text Critical Notes

Of v. 31[a-a] many scholars are in accord with BHS to construe the words *and with the house of Judah* as a late insertion, citing its absence from v. 33.[203] In v. 32[ac] both pronouns, הֵ֫מָּה and אָנֹכִ֫י, are used as subject to finite verbs. This implies that they have an emphatic force.[204] With regard to v. 32[b] the repeated noun

---

203 Keown, *Jeremiah 26-52, WBC*, 126; Carroll, *Jeremiah*, 610; Holladay, *Jeremiah 2*, 154.

204 T. Muraoka, *Emphatic Words and Structures in Biblical Hebrew* (Jerusalem: Magnes Press, 1985), 48.

has a retrospective function.[205] Of v. 32[d] the LXX reads καὶ ἐγὼ ἠμέλησα αὐτῶν, *and I abominated them.* Apparently the LXX has read *gā'alt'i* instead of *bā'alt'i.*[206] In the MT it means *despite Israel's breaking of the covenant, Yahweh is still their master.*[207] In v. 33[a] a few manuscripts read, ינב, *sons/children of.* MT's *house of* follows the diction of v. 31. Concerning v. 33[b] several manuscripts add waw consecutive to MT's perfect, יתתנו, *then I will put.*[208] LXX reads διδοὺς δώσω νόμους μου εἰς τὴν διάνοιαν αὐτῶν, *I certainly shall give my laws in their mind.* The verb נָתַן *to lay*, is rendered in its general meaning *to give.*[209] Of v. 33[c] The LXX has an aggravated translation of בְּקִרְבָּם *in their midst; within them.* The phrase can be taken literally *in their interior* meaning *in the heart of their city.*[210] Regarding v. 34[a] the LXX has a singular, while the imperative in the MT is in plural. In v. 34[b] the LXX has a zero-variant for *oracle of Yahweh.*[211] Of v. 34[c] the לְ in לַעֲוֹנָם is to be construed as indicating the object.[212]

5.2. Jeremiah 31:31-34 as Part of the Book of Consolation

Jeremiah 30-31 is commonly called *The Book of Comfort* or *The Book of Consolation.*[213] According to T. Collins,

> Jer 31:31-34 is not a text on its own, but embedded in a literary context. From a composition-critical point

205 P. Joüon & T. Muraoka, *A Grammar of Biblical Hebrew*, 2d ed. Subsidia Biblica, 27 (Rome: Editrice Pontificio Istituto Biblico, 2006), 158h.

206 E. Tov, *Textual Criticism of the Hebrew Bible,* 2nd rev. ed. (Minneapolis: Fortress Press, 1992), 236-258.

207 Bob Becking, "Text-Internal and Text-External Chronology in Jeremiah 31:31-34," *SEA* 61 (1996): 35-36.

208 Keown, *Jeremiah 26-52, WBC*, 154.

209 Becking, "Text-Internal and Text-External Chronology in Jeremiah 31:31-34," *SEA:* 36.

210 Holladay, *Jeremiah 2*, 1989.

211 Becking, "Text-Internal and Text-External Chronology in Jeremiah 31:31-34," *SEA:* 36-37.

212 Joüon, *A Grammar of Biblical Hebrew*, 125k.

213 Miller, "The Book of Jeremiah," *NIB:* 797.

of view, one could argue that the whole of the book of Jeremiah should be considered as the co-text of Jer 31:31-34.[214]

From a literary-critical point of view opposite observations have been made. Holladay and many others regard Jer 31:31-34 as part of a later redaction when words from the early career of Jeremiah originally directed to the remnant of the Northern Kingdom were reapplied to the South.[215] Other scholars construe Jer 31:31-34 as a deuteronomistic intrusion into the Book of Consolation.[216] Becking is of the view that literary-critical operations into and redaction-critical observations regarding a textual unit can only be made after a thorough structural reading of the text. Otherwise, presuppositions will take the lead in the literary-critical enterprise.[217] Therefore, it is more adequate to regard the Book of Consolation as the primary co-text.

5.3. The Context of Jeremiah 30-31

Jeremiah's book of comfort or consolation is born out of the concrete context of sixth century BCE where the dawn of Babylonian exile is the context in which the Jewish community lived. This hope proclaimed by Jeremiah is candid in all its dimensions about the real struggles of life.[218] According to Brueggemann, the chapters are a powerful statement of hope made to the exiles, announcing that the exile will come to an end because God intends to bring the community back to its own land. The God who willed exile now wills homecoming. The God who plucks up and tears down is the very God who will now plant and build (cf. Jer 1:10; 31:28). Exile is not a defeat or

214 T. Collins, *The Mantle of Elijah: The Redaction Criticism of the Prophetical Books* (Sheffield: JSOT Press 1993), 104-124.

215 Holladay, *Jeremiah 2*, 160.

216 Nicholson, *Preaching to the Exiles*, 82-85.

217 Becking, "Text-Internal and Text-External Chronology in Jeremiah 31:31-34," *SEA:* 37.

218 Jesurathnam, *Exploring Dalit Liberative Hermeneutics in India & the World*, 292.

failure for God, but the arena out of which God works a glorious newness for God's beloved people and for God's treasured city.[219]

For Dumbrell, the message of the book of Jeremiah is that the time of the Gentiles has arrived with the hegemony of Babylon over the ancient world. The end of the political history of Israel has thus virtually come. The facts of the exile will bear this out. Therefore, the political connections established with Israel by covenant thus stood in need at this time of theological restatement.[220]

5.4. The Question of Authenticity

There is no consensus among scholars regarding the authenticity of the passage. The division exists between those who accept them as the crown of Jeremiah's authentic preaching, and those who consider them to be post-Jeremianic and who belittle them. The first and most vigorous opponent of its authenticity was Duhm.[221] Cornill, Moulton and others were quick to reject this approach, and most scholars would agree with them. Bright, for example, thinks that the case need no longer be argued *it ought never to have been questioned.*[222] Herrmann and Nicholson have taken a mediating position, accepting the value of the passage, but denying its ascription to Jeremiah.[223] von Rad distinguishes between the attempt of the Deuteronomists to re-establish Israel on the old basis and the new conception here. With this Martin-Achard

---

219 Brueggemann, *A Commentary on Jeremiah: Exile and Homecoming,* 270.

220 Dumbrell, *Covenant and Creation*, 173.

221 J. Swetnam, "Why was Jeremiah's New Covenant New?" *SVT* 26 (1974): 111-115.

222 W. J. Moulton, "The New Covenant in Jeremiah," *The Expositor*, Series 7,1 (1906): 370-382; Bright, *Jeremiah*, 287; John Bright, "An Exercise in Hermeneutics Jeremiah 31:31-34," *Interpretation* 20 (1966): 188-210; John Bright, *Covenant and Promise: The Prophetic Understanding of the Future in Pre-Exilic Israel* (London: Westminster Press, 1976), 194.

223 Nicholson, *Preaching to the Exiles*, 82.

agrees.[224] M. Weinfeld would agree that Jeremiah's conception is distinctly different from that of Deuteronomy and reflects "a certain disappointment with the literary-religious activity which failed to improve the spiritual attitude of the people."[225] The whole point of these verses is that they are a deliberate contrast to Deuteronomy, not a complement to it, or a restatement of it.

5.5. Form and Structure of Jeremiah 31:31-34

The Book of Consolation concludes with a series of five short salvation oracles. The five oracles form a chiasm centered on Jer 31:31–34, the promise of the new covenant. The first (Jer 31:23–26) and fifth (Jer 31:38–40) oracles are about Jerusalem. The second (Jer 31:27–30) and fourth (Jer 31:35–37) form a contrasting pair.[226] These oracles also supplement, explain, and draw out the implications of the primarily poetic compositions that precede them in Jer 30–31. They are more consistently future oriented than the rest of the Book of Consolation, and they refer to the recipients of the promises in the third person throughout.[227] The prophecy on the *new covenant* (Jer 31:31-34) is part of the second textual unit introduced by הִנֵּה יָמִים בָּאִים, 'see, the days are coming' (Jer 31:31-37). This unit contains two smaller units. Jer 31:35-37 function as a motivation for vv. 31-34. This function can be formulated in a thematic way as follows: The reliability of reality underscores the reliability of the promise.[228]

From a syntactical point of view, Jer 31:31-34 is a complex text. Becking is of the view that Jer 31:31-34 can be construed as

224 G. von Rad, *Old Testament Theology: The Theology of Israel's Prophetic Traditions,* vol. 2, trans. D. M. G. Stalker (Edinburgh & London: Oliver & Boyd, 1965), 212.

225 Weinfeld, "Jeremiah and the Spiritual Metamorphosis of Israel," *ZAW*: 17-56.

226 Keown, *Jeremiah 26-52, WBC*, 126.

227 B. Bozak, *Life 'Anew:' A Literary-Theological Study of Jer. 30-31*, Analecta Biblica 122: Roma: Gregorian Biblical Book Shop, 1991), 110.

228 Becking, "Text-Internal and Text-External Chronology in Jeremiah 31:31-34," *SEA:* 37.

containing one complex sentence built up from several clauses which relate to each other.[229] According to Holladay, the first half (vv. 31-33aα) is prose and the second (vv. 33aß- 34) poetry, but both halves are carefully organized. Thus, it begins and ends with *the days* and *those days*. Within those expressions are the references to the new covenant as well as references to the old covenant.[230]

5.6. Setting

According to J. Coleman Baker, the new covenant oracle was addressed to the people of Judah (and Israel) after the destruction of Jerusalem and the temple.[231] Blackwood maintains that this prophecy was given *when every visible evidence of the original covenant had been destroyed*, either around the time of the destruction of Jerusalem and the temple or shortly thereafter during the early exile,[232] perhaps, according to Holladay, at 'the recitation of Deuteronomy in Jerusalem at the festival of booths in September/October 587 BCE.' Such a recitation would be approximately two months after the fall of the city in July (Jer 39:2) and a month after the temple was burned (2 Kings 25:8-9). It is not at all unlikely that such an observance would have taken place. The destruction of the main buildings of the city and the associated deportation of the leading citizens would have been for Jeremiah evidence for the end of the reality of the covenant mediated by Moses; it makes appropriate an announcement of Yahweh's fresh work for the people in time to come.[233]

---

229 Becking, "Text-Internal and Text-External Chronology in Jeremiah 31:31-34," *SEA:* 37.

230 Holladay, *Jeremiah 2*, 164-165.

231 J. Coleman Baker, "New Covenant, New Identity: A Social-Scientific Reading of Jeremiah 31:31-34," *The Bible and Critical Theory*, 4/1 (2008): 5.1.

232 A. W. Blackwood, *Commentary on Jeremiah* (Waco: Word, 1977), 58.

233 Holladay, *Jeremiah 2*, 165.

5.7. Explanation

5.7.1. In What Sense is the New Covenant New? (v. 31)

The short passage which develops form the simple announcement in this verse is one of the most important in the book of Jeremiah. Thompson asserts that it *represents one of the deepest insights in the whole OT.*[234] This prophecy has also been called one of the most profound and moving texts in the Bible,[235] towering *above any previous prophetic prediction.*[236]

5.7.1.1. Meaning of Days

Simon J. de Vries categorizes this form as a temporal introductory formula that is used almost exclusively by Amos and Jeremiah. This particular form introduces *radically altered, permanent conditions* for the hearers. The plural noun יָמִים is used here since this phrase is meant to introduce *a new, ongoing condition or situation that is predicated, not a singular event.*[237] This new condition has not yet, however, been realised. Werner Lemke asserts that the opening phrase points to some unspecified time in the future. It is found very frequently in the Jeremiah tradition, where it appears to be chiefly editorial in character and can refer both to times of judgment as well as to times of salvation. It obviously refers to a time of salvation.[238] Adeyemi notes that the anathrous יָמִים stress *the indefiniteness of the time of this*

234 Thompson, *The Book of Jeremiah, NICOT,* 580.

235 Bright, *Jeremiah, AB*, 287. See also Ronald E. Clements, *Jeremiah, Interpretation* (Atlanta: John Knox, 1988), 189; Carroll, *Jeremiah: A Commentary*, 612; Brueggemann, *A Commentary on Jeremiah: Exile and Homecoming*, 291.

236 von Rad, *Old Testament Theology*, 212.

237 S. J. de Vries, *From Old Revelation to New: A Tradition-Historical and Redaction-Critical Study of Temporal Transitions in Prophetic Prediction* (Grand Rapids: Eerdmans, 1995), 78.

238 Werner E. Lemke, "Jeremiah 31:31-34," *Interpretation* 37 (1983), 183.

covenant.[239] Hence, this new covenant *is a future expectation not a present reality.*[240]

5.7.1.2. The Concept of New Covenant

To *make a covenant* is literally *cut (כרת) a covenant*, which reflects the normal terminology of the OT. A covenant is a formal agreement, often established as firm by some kind of oath or promise. There is often some sign given to mark it as well.[241] For Keown, it is an act accomplished at a particular point in history. As such, it is a divine deed that can be promised for some time in the future.[242]

5.7.1.3. New Covenant

The Book of Consolation is filled with messages of hope for a future restoration of the Israelites to their land. These messages come to a climax at the end of chapter 31 with the proclamation of a new covenant. Exactly what is meant by the term *new* (חָדָשׁ) has been the subject of much scholarly debate. In the OT, the word *new* is used in a number of ways. The adjective חָדָשׁ occurs attributively 49 times in the OT,[243] and in most instances, it can refer to something which is of recent origin, unknown, unheard of, or never having been used or seen before (e.g., Ex 1:8; Deut 32:17; I Sam 6:7). It can mean in the sense of brand *new* or *novel.* On the other hand, *new* may also be used to refer to something which was known previously but which has received *renewed*

239 F. Adeyemi, *The New Covenant Torah in Jeremiah and the Law of Christ in Paul* (New York: Peter Lang, 2006), 45.

240 W. McKane, *A Critical and Exegetical Commentary on Jeremiah* (Edinburg: T&T Clark, 1986), 817. See also Tiberius Rata, *The Covenant Motif in Jeremiah's Book of Comfort: Textual and Intertextual Studies of Jeremiah 30-33* (New York: Peter Lang, 2007), 33.

241 Barclay M. Newman and Philip C. Stine, *A Handbook on Jeremiah* (New York : United Bible Societies, 2003), 651.

242 Keown, *Jeremiah 26-52, WBC,* 131.

243 Pieter A. Verhoef, "חָדָשׁ," *NIDOTTE*, ed. Willem A. VanGemeren (Grand Rapids: Zondervan, 1997), 30-37.

vitality or validity where the poet asserts that Yahweh's gracious mercy and compassion are *new* (*hâdàshim*) every morning. Lemke argues that *new* here cannot mean *novel* or *unheard of before*.[244] In the immediate context of this chapter, the same adjective occurs in v. 22 where it is used in conjunction with the verb to *create* (Heb. *bara'*) to indicate a totally new set of circumstances. One would surmise therefore that a radical discontinuity with the past is attached to the adjective in Jeremiah 31:31.[245] Yet the Greek OT translates Heb. *hadash* by Gk. καινός at this point, using an adjective referring to a qualitatively new dimension being added to the covenant experience and not merely or necessarily to a totally new divine initiative having no temporal reference to the past.[246] The TDNT states that *kainos* is "what is new in nature, different from the usual, impressive, better than the old, superior in value or attraction."[247] Walter Kaiser elaborates that "*νέος* refers to something brand new or distinctive in time or origin, often lacking maturity. *Kainos*, on the other hand, refers to what is new in nature, better than the old or superior in value or attraction."[248] Some maintain that there will be no difference in the covenant itself, rather in the manner in which it is observed. According to this viewpoint, as Sarason asserts, the new covenant is 'not a new *Torah*...just differently transmitted and more perfectly observed.'[249] On the contrary, Adeyemi maintains that the new covenant is *categorically contrasted with the Sinaitic Covenant* since the forgiveness of sins is promised in the new covenant and there were no 'stipulations regarding atonement and procedure for

244 Lemke, "Jeremiah 31:31-34," 186.

245 Dumbrell, *Covenant and Creation*, 175.

246 Dumbrell, *Covenant and Creation*, 175.

247 Johannes Behm, "καινός,j" *TDNT*, vol. III, ed. Gerhard Kittel, trans. Geoffrey W. Bromiley (Grand Rapids: Eerdmans, 1965), 447-450.

248 Walter C. Kaiser, "The Old Promise and the New Covenant: Jeremiah 31:31-34," *JETS* 15 (1972): 17.

249 R. S. Sarason, "The Interpretation of Jeremiah 31:31-34 in Judaism," *When Jesus and Christians Meet*, ed. Petuchowski (J. J. Albany: State University of New York Press, 1988), 105.

forgiveness of sin found in the Mosaic Law.'[250] Dumbrell rightly concludes:[251]

> There is thus continuity in the arrangement under consideration since the association of Yahweh with Israel will continue, but there is a radical discontinuity as well, since a new element is introduced which has not so far been part of Israel's experience. The relative balance of these two factors in the new covenant must be assessed.

Therefore, there seems to be a sense of continuity[252] as well as discontinuity[253] between the promised new covenant and the former covenants.

5.7.1.4. With Whom is the New Covenant Made?

One of the more interesting aspects of this passage is the stated recipients of the new covenant. The new covenant will be made with the *house of Israel and the house of Judah.* While some asserts that *house of David* in this verse may be an editorial expansion, Becking notes that there is no textual evidence of such an addition.[254] Adeyemi asserts that these two phrases always refer to *national state*.[255] The apparatus in the MT affirms that a few manuscripts contain *children of Israel* rather than *house of Israel*. Although a minority reading, the textual variation corresponds with the hope for a future united Israel that is present in the other Major Prophets and perhaps in the new covenant passage as

250 Adeyemi, *The New Covenant Torah in Jeremiah and the Law of Christ in Paul*, 74.

251 Dumbrell, *Covenant and Creation,* 175.

252 Lemke, "Jeremiah 31:31-34," 186.

253 Lemke, "Jeremiah 31:31-34," 186.

254 Blackwood, *Commentary on Jeremiah*, 227.

255 Adeyemi, *The New Covenant Torah in Jeremiah and the Law of Christ in Paul*, 48.

well.[256] Dumbrell is of the opinion that the *house of Judah* is often regarded as an editorial addition because only the *house of Israel* appears in v. 33. According to Dumbrell,[257]

> The twin reference to the existing geographical divisions of Israel and Judah in v. 31 recognizes the realities of the present national position or the position as it has existed since the division of the united kingdom into two entities after the death of Solomon. The new covenant will heal this breach....The point that Jeremiah is making here is a common exilic emphasis. There can be only one people of God and this concept will be exhibited in an inner harmony transcending the present geographical divisions.

5.7.2. Continuity and Discontinuity of the New Covenant (v. 32)

The background of this announcement is the covenant inaugurated between Yahweh and Israel at Sinai (Ex 19:1-24:11). The continued existence of the covenant depended on the continuing recognition of Yahweh as Lord, and continuing obedience to the terms of the covenant (Jer 11:1-8). Failure to obey these laws would result in judgment and the operation of the curses of the covenant. Obedience brought the covenant blessings.[258]

5.7.2.1. Not Like the Old Covenant

This new covenant or bond will differ from the Sinaitic Covenant, for God stated that it will "not [be] like the covenant which I made with their fathers in the day I took them . . . out of the land of Egypt." This new bond will exceed other known covenants in

256 Adeyemi Baker, "New Covenant, New Identity: A Social-Scientific Reading of Jeremiah 31:31-34," 5.8.

257 Dumbrell, *Covenant and Creation,* 175.

258 Thompson, *The Book of Jeremiah*, 580.

the AWA.[259] The new covenant will not be like the covenant that the Lord made with Israel's and Judah's ancestors of the exodus generation. The new covenant will be cut with a later generation who will have undergone spiritual return and geographical removal from a different place of captivity (Jer 31:15-22; 50:4-5). The former covenant had been broken (פרר *hiphil*) by the exodus ancestors, by Jeremiah's audience, and by all the generations in between.[260]

5.7.3. Place of Law in the New Covenant (v. 33)

5.7.3.1. House of Israel

The promise unites the two houses of v. 31 into the one *house of Israel*. Clements finds *house of Israel* significant as a new title for the people scattered in diaspora.[261] *After those days* in v. 33 indicates sequence, a later time, but does not specify the antecedent. It cannot be a time after the covenant making in v. 31, unless there are two such occasions envisioned. Rudolph identifies *those days*, v. 33, as the time of the promised return of Ephraim.[262] In the present context of the Book of Consolation, *those days* could mean the days described in Jer 30:27-30 when the judgment will be complete and God will begin planting, building, and repopulating the land.[263]

5.7.3.2. Law

There is no consensus among the scholars regarding the prophetic assertion of the *law* (*torah*). The most common view on the

---

259 McCarthy, "Covenant in the Old Testament: The Present State of Inquiry," *CBQ*: 238; see also M. Weinfeld, "The Covenant of Grant in the Old Testament and in the Ancient Near East," *Journal of the American Oriental Society* 90 (1970): 185. Renald E. Showers, *There Really Is a Difference: A Comparison of Covenant and Dispensational Theology* (Bellmawr, NJ: Friends of Israel, 1990), 102.

260 Keown, *Jeremiah 26-52, WBC*, 131.

261 Clements, *Jeremiah*, 191.

262 W. Rudolph, *Jeremia* (Tübingen: Mohr, Siebeck, 1968), 188.

263 Keown, *Jeremiah 26-52, WBC*, 132.

identity of the new covenant *torah* is that of John Calvin, a view also held by most covenant theologians today.

> For God does not say here, I will give you another Law/ but I will write my Law, that is, the same Law, which had formally been delivered to the Fathers. He then does not promise anything different as to the essence of the doctrine, but he makes the difference to be in the form only.[264]

In support of this view von Rad says the Mosaic Law still stands in the center of the new covenant and that Jeremiah never announced that God's revelation given at Sinai would be nullified *in whole or part.*[265] Clements agrees that Jeremiah simply envisaged "only a new way of Israel's knowing and keeping the existing law of the covenant made on Sinai...the central attention [being] upon the willingness to obey the known law."[266]

Other writers like Frank H. Seilhamer say the Law in Jer 31:33 differs from the *torah* of Sinai, which Israel was unable to keep because of human sinfulness. Jeremiah envisioned the new covenant as *rising out of the total destruction of the covenant made at Sinai*,[267] and he therefore did not envision a return of the

---

264 John Calvin, *Commentaries on the Book of the Prophet Jeremiah and Lamentations*, vol. 4, trans. John Owen (Edinburgh: Calvin Translation Society, 1850; reprint, Grand Rapids: Eerdmans, 1950), 131-32; and John Calvin, *Institutes of the Christian Religion*, trans. Ford Lewis Battles (Philadelphia: Westminster, 1971), 2.10.2.

265 von Rad, *Old Testament Theology*, 213.

266 Clements, *Jeremiah*, 191; See also Walter C. Kaiser Jr., *Toward Rediscovering the Old Testament* (Grand Rapids: Zondervan, 1987), 25-26; Walter C. Kaiser Jr., *Toward an Old Testament Theology* (Grand Rapids: Zondervan, 1978), 231-235; Walter C. Kaiser Jr., "The Law as God's Gracious Guidance for the Promotion of Holiness," *Five Views on Law and Gospel*, 189, 304; and Oswald T. Allis, *Prophecy and the Church* (Philadelphia: Presbyterian and Reformed, 1945), 42.

267 Frank H. Seilhamer, *The New Covenant in Jeremiah 31:31-34 and its Place in the Covenant-Treaty Tradition of Israel and the Ancient Near East* (Springfield, OH: New World, 1976), 3.

old law.[268] In this view Jeremiah's new covenant, having annulled the old covenant, awaits *new laws.*[269]

5.7.3.3. Uniqueness of New Covenant

This verse describes the unique difference of the new covenant.[270] H. W. Wolff says the first *completely new element* in the new covenant is the manner in which God's guiding directions would be mediated.[271] Rather than on tables of stone (Ex 31:18; Deut 4:13), God promised to write the law on *minds* (*qereb*, better *inmost being*, a more general term than *heart*[272]) and *hearts* (cf. Jer 17:1-2; Rom 7:4-6; 2 Cor 3:3, 6-16). The radical nature of this change is emphasized elsewhere by speaking of a *new heart* and a *new spirit* (Ezek 18:31; 36:26; cf. Ezek 11:19; Jer 24:7; 32:39).

Those under the new covenant will obey God not out of duty or fear but out of a God-given desire and ability to do so (cf. Rom 8:1-4; 2 Cor 5:14).[273] Thus, there would be no more need to modify the covenant, since Israel would no longer be breaking it (Jer 3:17); it is to be everlasting (Jer 32:40). As Brueggemann writes, "Obeying will be as normal and as readily accepted as

---

268 Charles H. Talbert, "Paul on the Covenant," *Review and Expositor* 84 (1987), 299-300

269 Edmond Jacob, *Theology of the Old Testament*, trans. Arthur W. Heathcote and Philip J. Allcock (New York: Harper and Brothers, 1958), 274.

270 See the discussion of what was new about the new covenant in Kaiser, Jr., *Toward an Old Testament Theology*, 231–35; Huey, *Jeremiah, Lamentations, NAC,* 284.

271 H. W. Wolff, *Confrontations with Prophets* (Philadelphia: Fortress, 1983), 54.

272 R. L. Harris, G. L. Archer, & B. K. Waltke, *Theological Wordbook of the Old Testament* (Chicago: Moody Press, 1980), 813.

273 J. G. McConville, "Jeremiah: Prophet and Book," *Tyndale Bulletin* 42 (1991): 93; G. von Rad says, "What is here outlined is the picture of a new man, a man who is able to obey perfectly because of a miraculous change of his nature." von Rad, *Old Testament Theology*, 213-14.

breathing and eating...All inclination to resist, refuse, or disobey will have evaporated."[274]

5.7.3.4. Covenant Formula

With a new *heart*, God and the people will again be in relationship. The covenant formula, *I will be their God, and they shall be my people* is again right at the centre. Rolf Rendtorff is of the opinion that the decisive point is that it will be Israel's heart in which the knowledge of God is located.[275] The covenant formula occupies a central position between the declaration that the *torah*, as content of the covenant, will be written into the hearts of the Israelites and the other declaration that they will all know God without any external help (v. 34). The first part of the formula, *I will be their God*, follows the announcement that God will put his *torah* in their hearts; the second part, *and they shall be my people*, is followed by the declaration that they will all know God.

5.7.4. Framework of the New Covenant (v. 34)

Verse 34 begins with Heb. עֹוד... וְלֹא (*and no longer*), indicating by the w^e (Heb. *and*) an affirmation of the material of v. 33 and a continuance of it. With the *no longer* of the verse may presume the emergence of a new situation. There is emphasis in v. 34 on the immediacy of the new relationship. No longer will there be the need to preserve the instructional framework in which intermediaries such as priests and particularly prophets had operated under the old covenant. In the new situation all will know God, for knowledge will be direct and totally personal.[276]

5.7.4.1. Knowledge of Yahweh

A consequence of the new covenant will be that at last all the people will *know God*. Bracke asserts that *knowledg*e in the book of Jeremiah is not about an intellectual discernment of some fact

274 W. Brueggemann, *To Build, To Plant: A Commentary on Jeremiah 26–52* (Grand Rapids: Eerdmans, 1991), 71.

275 Rendtorff, *The Covenant Formula,* 34.

276 Dumbrell, *Covenant and Creation*, 181.

about God; rather, to *know* God meant to be devoted to God and to obey God. Israel and Judah, according to Jeremiah, were neither devoted to God nor did they obey. Jer 31:31-34 looks toward that day when God has established a new covenant and corrected the *heart* problem of the people so all will *know* God.[277] Wolff has urged, *knowledge of Yahweh* denotes a cognitive capacity to recite the saving traditions (Jer 2:6-8).[278] For Brueggemann, *knowledge of Yahweh* means affirmation of Yahweh as sovereign Lord with readiness to obey the commands for justice that is the will of Yahweh. Thus when Jer 22:15-17 speaks of *knowing Yahweh*, it suggests obedience to God's commands for justice.[279]

5.7.4.2. The Least to the Greatest

Knowledge of God will extend to all ages and classes.[280] The phrase *from the least to the greatest of them* sums up a list of people from children to the very aged in Jer 6:11–13. Although, it lacks this phrase, Jer 5:1–5 serves as background because it describes a situation that will be eradicated by this promise: neither poor nor rich *know the way of the Lord or the law of their God.* The same phrase, but without pronominal suffixes, describes the lay participants in the covenant renewal led by Josiah in 2 Kings 23:2 (cf. the list in Deut 29:9-10).[281] According to Brueggemann,

> There will be common, shared access to this knowledge which evidences fundamental egalitarianism in the community. On the crucial matter of connection to God, the least and the greatest stand on equal footing. No one has superior, elitist access, and no one lacks what is required. All share fully in the new relation.

---

277 John M. Bracke, *Jeremiah 30-52 and Lamentations, Westminster Bible Companion* (Louisveill, Kentucky: Westinster John Knox Press, 2000), 23.

278 Wolff, *Confrontations with Prophets*, 49-62.

279 Brueggemann, *A Commentary on Jeremiah: Exile and Homecoming,* 293.

280 Holladay, *Jeremiah 2*,198-199.

281 Keown, *Jeremiah 26-52*, 135.

> All know the story, all accept the sovereignty, and all embrace the commands.[282]

5.7.4.3. Forgiveness and Remember Sin No More

According to Dumbrell, the final and important factor which controls the era of the new covenant, Jeremiah tells us, is that it is the era of the forgiveness of sins, to be so extensive that God will not need to act against them.[283] The phrase is introduced by *ki*, as though this line states the basis for all the foregoing.[284] In the new age sin will not be required to be dealt with at all. This is a supposition of unfettered mutual fellowship between God and human beings, the creation of a community in which not only is there no need for instruction, but no breach of fellowship occurs; no divisions within the new community are expected[285] because God has broken the vicious cycle of sin and punishment. It is this broken cycle that permits Israel to begin again at a different place with new possibility.[286] The promised new covenant rests upon God's decision to forgive and not remember sin. God's decision opens the possibility for restoration, for building and planting, for a new covenant and a fresh start between God and the people.[287] For Henk Leena, Jeremiah addresses the issue of restoration of Judah in a more comprehensive and in more personal terms that no one will be kept away from the plan of God for Judah. Every member of the community will receive individual forgiveness and that will become a basis for personal relationship with God.[288]

---

282 Brueggemann, *A Commentary on Jeremiah: Exile and Homecoming,* 294.

283 Dumbrell, *Covenant and Creation*, 182.

284 Brueggemann, *A Commentary on Jeremiah: Exile and Homecoming,* 294.

285 Dumbrell, *Covenant and Creation*, 182.

286 Brueggemann, *A Commentary on Jeremiah: Exile and Homecoming,* 294.

287 Bracke, *Jeremiah 30-52 and Lamentations*, 23.

288 Henk Leena, *Newness in Old Testament Prophecy: An Intertextual Study* (Leiden-Boston: Brill, 2014), 205.

Conclusion

From the above observation, we can summarize the findings of the chapter with the following points.

First, Jeremiah 31:31-34 proposes a new covenant to replace Yahweh's covenant with Israel at the time of Egyptian exodus. What is announced here is a new beginning and just as elsewhere Israel is once again to experience a new exodus from bondage. In terms of stipulations the new covenant does not differ from the old in many respects. Both the covenants put their emphases on the people's obedience to *torah*. But, there were a shift and change in Jeremiah that God will write his *torah* on their hearts so that everyone will be attuned to it.[289] Hence, there is a sense of continuity and discontinuity between the old and the new covenant.

Second, what is new in this restoration plan of God is thus understood in terms of God takes care of the needs of each individual and giving the freedom for every individual to make their choice so that the community at the end will be altogether restored.[290] This teaching of the new covenant will be very relevant to the contemporary context of Mizoram.

Third, to build and plant is the main phrase that was repeatedly used by the prophet in the midst of tearing down and plucking up. God's judgment has totally shattered the people and exposed them to reality of their situation. The people of Judah can no longer boast of their cultic prowess and the royal Zion and Jerusalem's invincibility. In such a situation, the word of comfort or hope preached by Jeremiah is of tremendous significance and value.[291] Thus, this word of hope is also visible in the new covenant and it is presented in the context of Israel's future hope.

---

289 Jesurathnam, *Exploring Dalit Liberative Hermeneutics in India & the World*, 299.

290 Jesurathnam, *Exploring Dalit Liberative Hermeneutics in India & the World*, 300.

291 Jesurathnam, *Exploring Dalit Liberative Hermeneutics in India & the World*, 300.

Fourth, what is clear in Jer 31:31-34 is the theocentric character of the new covenant. We find a series of first person divine addresses during the course of the verses. Therefore, God is at the center and from the beginning to the end the new covenant rests upon divine initiative, and is constituted by a divine pardon which permits a new beginning.

Fifth, this new covenant is to be made (v. 31) with the *house of Israel* and *with the house of Judah*. It will heal the breach between the two houses and joined together the geographical divisions; it will create a new and inclusive community without any division. Therefore, it can be argued that the intention of the new covenant is to create a new community or an inclusive community. God's decision opens the possibility for restoration, for building and planting, for a new covenant and a fellowship between God and the people.

Sixth, the prophetic assertion of the new covenant is full of ethical teachings. There will be knowledge of Yahweh which is based on justice and righteousness. There will be common, shared access to this knowledge which evidences fundamental egalitarianism in the community. God will forgive their iniquities and remember their sins no more. Thus, the message of the new covenant will have implications for contemporary context in Mizoram.

Finally, this passage is seen by Christians as a messianic prophecy fulfilled in Jesus.[292] Jeremiah promised new covenant to the fractured community but its fulfilment was not yet observed during his time. As such, the NT understanding of the new covenant will bring a shift and change. It will also draw implications for the Church and community in Mizoram.

292 Kizhakkeyil, *Jeremiah: An Exegetical Commentary*, 187.

Chapter 6

A Tribal Reading on the New Covenant Motif and Its Implication for Mizo Society

Introduction

The researcher has dealt with the selected passage in the previous chapter and the analysis of the text implies that the central and primary motif of the new covenant in Jeremiah is based on the ethical teaching that will have implication for the contemporary community. What is new here is that it will not be like the old ones but offers new community and alternate community marked by justice and righteousness, egalitarianism, communitarianism and forgiveness. Jeremiah announced a new beginning that God will take care of the needs and freedom of each individual so that the community at the end will altogether be restored. It also offers hope and comfort for the fractured community who are in a desperate situation.

Further, the new covenant motif does not end in the OT but continues through the NT. It is, therefore, necessary to engage in the NT understanding of the new covenant. Thus, we need to examine the following questions: What is the NT understanding of the new covenant? Was it different from the understanding of Jeremiah? How they are interrelated? How did Jesus fulfil the new covenant mentioned in Jeremiah? Another question needed to be asked are: What are the characteristic features of the new covenant? What are its ethical frameworks? How far the new covenant text can be appropriated for the socio-economic, political and ecclesiastical condition in Mizoram? What are its implications for the ethical life of the community and Church in Mizoram?

6.1. New Covenant in the NT

The early Christian Church understood itself to be the people of the new covenant and claimed the promise of Jer 31:31–34. It also thought of itself as a new people (1 Pet 2:1-10). It was surprising to find so little said in the NT about a new covenant[293] though in the broader sense the concerns of covenant are embedded in the theological thinking of the NT. Jesus' words of new covenant are found only in the text of Lk 22:20. At the Last Supper Jesus passes the wine and says, *This cup...is the new covenant in my blood.* Scholarly opinion is divided about the originality of this reading, though the longer text does have wide support.[294] The text ignores the question whether God has already fulfilled the new covenant promise in the life of the Second Temple Israel and uses the image

293 G. E. Wright attributes the paucity of references to legalistic connotations which the term "covenant" had in the NT period. He says "covenant" had come to mean almost exclusively obedience to the law; for this reason NT writers were uncomfortable with the term, using it only to point out that in Christ the covenant was not law but faith or life in the Spirit. NT rhetoric at this point contrasts sharply with Jewish rhetoric and rhetoric found in the Essene sectarian documents from Qumran. Lundbom, "New Covenant," *ABD*: 1090.

294 In some ancient manuscripts both the Mark and Matthew texts have the word *new* added. Some form-critics conclude that neither *new* nor *covenant* was spoken by Jesus, which is to say the Last Supper liturgy was originally more brief and in each of the synoptic passages has undergone expansion. R. Bultmann. *Theology of the New Testament.* 2 vols., translated by K. Grobel (Texas: Baylor University Press, 2007), 146.

of a new covenant to interpret the significance of Jesus' death.[295] Patrick D. Miller remarked:[296]

> The very expression *New Testament* serves to identify the new covenant with the Christ-event. The further identification of the blood of Christ and the cup of communion with the *new covenant* (Lk 22:20; 1 Cor 11:25) serves to underscore the NT claim to perceive the establishment of new covenant relationship in the advent of Christ and the creation of community that defines its relationship to God through Jesus Christ. The reference to the blood of Christ is a way of pointing to the divine act of salvation that redeems a people by God's own power and grace.

Christians know that particularly in the cross and celebrate it. Just as the exodus event is a pointer to Christ event, so also the latter is a confirmation of the other. Some of the NT texts go further in seeing the new covenant in Christ as a negation of the old covenant with Israel (e.g., 2 Cor 3:5-14; Heb 8:8-12; 10:16-17). According to Miller, "Christians probably need to hear these texts both critically and appreciatively. This is the way we are drawn into the covenant, as members of a community of the new covenant. However God's covenant is renewed with Israel, the Christian community enters anew to that new covenant through Christ."[297] The largest question about the new covenant is not about who belongs to it but about whether any of us, Jew or Christian, show forth the new heart and new spirit that God has promised to effect within us.

295 Matthew's formulation (Mat 26:28) indicates the way in which this is a new covenant, because Jesus' death is of key significance for the forgiveness of the many, both Israel and the world. Goldingay, "Covenant, OT and NT," *NIDB*: 775.

296 Miller, "The Book of Jeremiah," *NIB:* 815.

297 Miller, "The Book of Jeremiah," *NIB:* 815-816.

In Pauline letters there are eight occurrences of covenant (*diathēkē*).[298] Paul refers to himself and the Corinthian laity as *ministers of a new covenant* (2 Cor 3:6) where Jer 31:31–34 appears to be in the back of his mind. This covenant has found expression in the hearts of the Corinthians, wherein the *Spirit of the living God* resides (2 Cor 3:2–3). It therefore contrasts with the *old covenant* of Moses (2 Cor 3:14–15) which was written on stone (2 Cor 3:3).[299] Goldingay rightly pointed out:

> Paul thus sees the new covenant as a present reality, though he can of course recognize that the process of transformation is incomplete; further, he cannot believe that God will never take away that veil. Thus he can also see the implementation of Jeremiah's new covenant as lying at the time when God's ultimate purpose is fulfilled and all Israel is saved (Rom 11:25-27).[300]

In the NT, the new covenant is given its most prominent place in the letter to the Hebrews. The new covenant passage from Jeremiah is quoted twice, once in its entirety (Heb 8:8–12) and once in abridged form (Heb 10:16–17).[301] In Hebrew, *Jesus is the mediator of a new covenant* by virtue of the fact that *a death has occurred that redeems them from the transgressions under the first covenant* (Heb 9:15). The old covenant with its shortcomings (Heb 8:7-8) is thus obsolete and about to disappear (Heb 8:13). The single definitive sacrifice that Christ offered makes the regular

---

298 Of special note among these are Gal 4:24 (two covenants), 2 Cor 3:6 (the only use in Paul of new covenant, *kainē diathēkē*, apart from the eucharistic passage in 1 Cor 11:25) and 2 Cor 3:14 where we find the only reference to old covenant, *palaia diathēkē*. W. S. Campbell, "Covenant and New Covenant," *Dictionary of Paul and His Letters*, eds. Gerald F. Hawthorne, Ralph P. Martin & Daniel G. Reid (Downers Grove, Illinois: InterVarsity Press, 1993), 179.

299 Lundbom, "New Covenant," *ABD*: 1091.

300 Goldingay, "Covenant, OT and NT," *NIDB*: 775.

301 Lundbom, "New Covenant," *ABD*: 1092.

sacrifices now unnecessary.[302] Therefore, as already promised by Jeremiah this new covenant is inaugurated by Jesus Christ. Jesus becomes the mediator of the new covenant by virtue of his death on the cross.

6.2. New Covenant as a Subversive Paradigm and Its Ethical Framework

The factors that pave the way for God's new covenant as a subversive paradigm and its ethical framework for the contemporary situation may be discussed as follows:

6.2.1. New Community/New Identity

God had built a community on earth by creating the subversive aspect in the covenant that was initiated with Israelites.[303] The promise of the new community on earth is made especially by Jeremiah (Jer 31:31). According to Brueggemann, it is important that Jeremiah, most anguished of the prophets, speaks this hope, for only one in anguish could hope so deeply. It is equally important that he speaks this anticipation precisely at a time of historical brokenness when there seems no ground for hope. The new community he anticipates is not to be derived from the old shattered one. It depends only and singularly on a new move from God, a response to groans. It is this move that makes possible what was not possible before the groans were received and embraced.[304] John Bright affirms that "it is a new covenant in that it is made anew, renewed; but it is the people who are

302 Whereas in the OT the sacrifice involved in confirming the covenant at Sinai was separate from the regular sacrificial system, Hebrews brings these two together; it can then see the covenant sacrifice as cleansing sacrifice (Heb 9:21-22). But the fact that Jer 31:34 speaks of forgiveness as still future shows that these cleansing sacrifices did not really *work*. Goldingay, "Covenant, OT and NT," *NIDB*: 775-776.

303 K. Jesurathnam, "Socio-Economic and Politico-Religious Horizons of Covenant Community of Israel: Some Ethical Implications," *MJT*, 4/2 (December, 2014): 37.

304 Brueggemann, *A Social Reading of the Old Testament*, 47.

made new."[305] Unterman also summarizes that "in this manner the new covenant will result in the creation of the ideal positive relationship between Yahweh and His people."[306] Therefore, the intention of the new covenant is to create a new community or an inclusive community.

6.2.2. Forgiveness

The mark of the new community envisioned is that it knows about, experiences, and practices forgiveness and it serves as antidote to disobedience. It could mean to be in right relationship with God who initiated the covenant. It is not simply a spiritual notion but includes a genuine redistribution of power. It also means forgiveness of debts as suggested in Mt 6:12, the end of bondage, the overcoming of social inequality.[307] In the NT forgiveness is the main teaching of Jesus. Jesus taught that if we forgive others, God will forgive us (Mt 6:14,15). In order to have a right relationship with God, the ethics of forgiveness is a key factor for the Mizo community and the Church.

6.2.3. Obedience to *Torah*

The new covenant community is committed to *torah* obedience. It is not an end to the law but readiness to be obedience to *torah* and its new meaning. This commitment to *torah* is filled with justice, mercy, compassion, and righteousness that will undergird all the covenant relations of the community. This covenant relationships within and outside the community is in contrast to the present one that is characterized by knowledge, power and wealth at the cost of the neighbour (cf. Jer 9:23-24).[308] Jesus also came not to abolish the law but to fulfill it (Mt 5:17-20). Therefore, we find the new meaning of *torah* in the teaching of Jesus and this commitment

---

305 Bright, *Covenant and Promise*, 196.

306 Jeremiah Unterman, *From Repentance to Redemption: Jeremiah's Thought in Transition*. JSOT Sup54 (Sheffield: Sheffield Academic, 1987), 102.

307 Brueggemann, *A Social Reading of the Old Testament*, 47-48.

308 Brueggemann, *A Social Reading of the Old Testament*, 48.

to *torah* has significant implications for the Church in Mizoram which is marked by justice, peace and compassion.

6.2.4. Knowledge of Yahweh

The new covenant community is also marked by the *knowledge of Yahweh*. Knowledge of God calls this community away from its many other knowledges that betray and divide. It means attentiveness to poor, needy people, the transformation of social relations and public institutions for the sake of justice. The least as well as the greatest shall know. The strong and the weak know together. The credentialed and the uncredentialed share the gift. The word to the strong in the community is that the weak ones also know the same. Within the church there are no monopolies of this knowledge, not by wealth or longevity or gender or anything else.[309] Jesus' teaching of the knowledge of Yahweh is found in the Nazareth Manifesto in Luke 4:16-21. Jesus came to bring good news to the poor and to let the captives free. The Church, particularly the Mizo Church, has an important mission to rescue the oppressed and uplift those who are in need.

6.2.5. Justice and Righteousness

According to Jeremiah, knowledge of God means doing justice and righteousness. To know God is to do social justice. The Hebrew word for knowing is *yada*. It means entering into deep relationship of personal commitment.[310] It involves a concern for the poor and the needy, practice of justice and righteousness and obeying covenant stipulations. The message of Jeremiah *to pluck and to pull down, to destroy and to overthrow, to build and to plant* (Jer 1:10) envisages the overthrowing of the unjust and corrupt structures of the society and the building up of a new society of justice and righteousness.[311] In the NT as well, the teaching of the new covenant is marked by justice and righteousness. Jesus

309 Brueggemann, *A Social Reading of the Old Testament*, 48.

310 D. R. Jones, *Jeremiah, NCB* (Grand Rapids: Eerdmans, 1992), 289-290.

311 Thomas Vallianippuram, "*Mispat* and *Sedaqa*: The Vision of Social Justice in Jeremiah," *Bible Bhashyam* 34/4 (2010), 321.

came to dismantle injustice and unjust practice. This teaching can be effectively connected to the contemporary community in Mizoram where injustice and unjust structures have done harm to the people.

6.2.6. Equality

The new covenant community is also marked by its egalitarian principle that the knowledge of God will be available from the least to the greatest in the community. This implies that under the new covenant the community will experience equality that no hierarchical ranking would exist and no group can dominate and monopolize the knowledge of God. In the NT, Paul vividly declares that all are one/equal and there is no caste or class division before Jesus Christ (Gal 3:28-29). In our contemporary context, there is an enormous gap that separate the rich and the poor. Equality is the need of an hour in which all are equal without any discrimination.

6.2.7. Solidarity and Communitarianism

Many commentators have tended to stress the individualism of the new covenant and to see in this singling out of the individual a major advance in religion initiated by Jeremiah. Individualism combined with inwardness of religion is the essential features of the new covenant. However, it needs to be emphasized that the covenant is made 'with the house of Israel and the house of Judah' (Jer 31:31) and not with individuals.[312] In the case of tribal and Mizo community, communitarianism is a concept and life principle in which equality of all is basic in their understanding of human being and more attention is given to the society than to the individual.[313] According to this concept, inclusiveness is

312 Carroll, *From Chaos to Covenant*, 221.

313 Vanlalchhuanawma & Rosiamliana Tochhawng, "Identification of Communalities and Divergence in Doing Theology from Tribal Perspective," *Dalit-Tribal Theological Interface: Current Trends in Subaltern Theologies*, eds. James Massey and Shimreingam Shimray (TSC/WSC: ETC Jorhat, 2007), 233.

a major concern and the community is open to the rest of the world. Therefore, this communitarian concept is crucial to build a just and harmonious community open for all and free from discrimination, where women, widows, poor and weaker section of the community have hopes for future emancipation and living with dignity.

6.2.8. Hope and Comfort

Jeremiah presented the new covenant in the context of Israel's future hope. He announced that God's plan of restoration is holistic, enduring, and comprehensive in every respect. In this new order, God is going to bring out the ordering of the lives of the community covers all spheres of life. The very fact that God forgives the iniquities of the people of Judah and remember their sins no more will create a new possibility that is hitherto unknown to the people.[314] Thus, the Jeremianic perspective of hope and reconstruction visualizes a new community and a new humanity in Christ. This message of hope will have implications for our contemporary context of pastoral care and counselling.

6.3. Its Implication for Mizo Tribal Community

It is true to say that Christianity and the Church have served the society in Mizoram. Had there been no Churches in Mizoram, the history of Mizoram would have been different from what it is now. In this context, it may not be an exaggeration to say that the Churches played role in the improvement or transformation of the socio-economic and political context in Mizoram, otherwise the Mizos would have been a lost tribe not known to anybody today

314 Eilliam Schweiker and Michael Welker, "A New Paradigm of Theological and Biblical Inquiry," *Power, Powerlessness and the Divine: New Inquiries in Bible and Theology*, ed. Cynthia L. Rigby (Atlanta: Scholars Press, 1997): 3-20, cited by Jesurathnam, *Exploring Dalit Liberative Hermeneutics in India & the World*, 310.

and the political unit known as Mizoram would never appear in the map of this country.[315]

6.3.1. Socio-Economic, Political and Religious Conditions of Mizoram

We cannot understand the situation of the Church without understanding the socio-political and religious condition of Mizoram.

6.3.1.1. Tribal Community - Identity Crisis

First of all, the Mizo people are categorized as tribal by the constitution of India. A. Wati Longchar terms the tribals as *A Defeated Community in India*. Their history is a history of defeat, suffering and oppression. In this globalized era, the tribals also became the victims of modernization.[316] In his description about the status of the tribals, K. Thanzauva laments: "They are culturally alienated, socially stigmatised, economically exploited, poor and politically powerless."[317] The identity given to the tribal by the Indian Constitution also clearly manifests the attitude of the dominant class of Indian society. According to Lalsangkima Pachuau, the identity given to the tribal is 'artificially constructed' for the convenience of the administrative system that is thoroughly influenced by the caste stratification mindset.[318]

Therefore, the constitutional identity of tribals has evolved out of the caste system, the mindset of which reduced them to a sub-human level in the society. Thus, the new covenant message of hope is very much appropriate for the Tribal people in Mizoram

---

315 H. Vanlalauva, "Role of the Churches in Mizoram," *MTJ*, 6/1 (January-June, 2006): 17.

316 A. Wati Longchar, "The Need for Studying Tribal Theology," *An Exploration of Tribal Theology*, ed. A. Wati Longchar (Jorhat: The Tribal Study Centre, 1997), 3.

317 K. Thanzauva, *Theology of Community* (Bangalore: Asian Trading Corporation, 2004), 11.

318 Lalsangkima Pachuau, ""Tribal" Identity and Ethnic Conflicts in Northeast India: A "Tribal" Christian Response," *BTF* XXXI/1 (July, 1999): 161.

who faced discrimination, oppression and alienation in their search for identity.

6.3.1.2. Political Condition

Since Mizoram was officially declared as a full-fledged state on 20th February 1987, many developments took place especially in the field of political system.[319] Political party system was introduced and people elected political leaders to rule over them.[320] Unfortunately party politics is misused and resulted in corruption which had a negative impact on the life of the people and the church as well. H. Lalrinthanga observed that the politicians and the Government officials are corrupt and they misuse public funds. With the growth of money economy, money power has been used to influence voters in the election. Politics is now completely commercialized and almost the entire fund benefited a few individuals at the cost of the general public.[321] Lalnithanga also asserts,

> There was practically a mad race in this direction in the process of which the moral code and ethics were altogether thrown into the wind resulting in the attempt and desire to acquire money by hook or by crook without any regard for the wholesomeness or otherwise of the means adopted for such purpose.[322]

319 Suhas Chatterjee, *Mizoram Under the British Rule* (New Delhi: Miltal Publications, 1985), 4; H. Lallungmuana, "Mizo Culture and Christianity," *Kum Za Mel Lung*, ed. Vanlalnghaka Ralte, et al. (Aizawl: Aizawl Theological College, 2007): 175; H. L. Malsawma, *Sociology of the Mizos* (Guwahati: Spectrum Publications, 2002), 14; C. G. Verghese and R. L. Thanzawna, *A History of the Mizos*, vol. 1 (New Delhi: Vikas Publishing House Pvt. Ltd., 1997), 39.

320 V. S. Lalrinawma, *Mizo Ethos: Changes and Challenges* (Aizawl: Mizoram Publication Board, 2005), 301.

321 H. Lalrinthanga, *Church and State: Relationship in the Mizo Socio-Political Life 1952 to 2006* (Delhi: ISPCK, 2013), 171.

322 P. Lalnithanga, *Emergence of Mizoram*, 2nd edition (Aizawl: P. Lalnithanga, 2005), 101.

Thus, corruption created the gap between the rich and the poor in every area of Mizo life. K. Lallawmzuala believed that the widened of the gap between the rich and the poor was because of the de-value of the old saying *sem sem dam dam, ei bil thi thi* (sharing you live, greedily eating you die).[323] The misconception on political ideology divides people and resulted in increasing corruption, bribery, favouritism, dishonesty, lies etc. Therefore, the ethical teaching of new covenant is relevant in a Mizo society in order to have an ideal Church and society where there are so many injustices while unjust structure has done harm to the people in the political arena.

6.3.1.3. Socio-Economic Condition

Today, the social life of the Mizo has been degraded by money economy. Nag observed that the introduction of education prepared the educated Mizo for a job oriented life and not for the *jhumming*.[324] People try to get as much money as they can from different sources in one way or the other which causes corruption and bribery in the society. All these things ruin Mizo society slowly.[325]

As mentioned above, communitarianism is a concept and the life principle of a Mizo tribal community in which the people live together sharing their joys and sorrows in mutual love and care.[326] One of the most important social-ethical principles or foundations of the Mizo community is called *tlawmngaihna*,[327] and *Zawlbuk*.[328] But, all those fine qualities of Mizo morality have been degraded. Lalmanzuala laments, "Honesty has been replaced by falsehood

---

323 K. Lallawmzuala, "Sem Sem Dam Dam, Ei Bil Thi Thi," *Hmatiang Sawnin* (Move Forward) (Bangalore: Shalom Publication, 2001), 288.

324 Chitta Rajan Nag, *Mizo Polity and Political Modernization* (Delhi: Vikash Publishing House Pvt. Ltd., 1988), 77.

325 Lalrinthanga, *Church and State*, 169.

326 Thanzauva, *Theology of Community*, 136.

327 Thanzauva, *Theology of Community*, 152.

328 J. Shakespeare, *The Lushai Kuki Clans* (Aizawl: Tribal Research Institute, 1912 (rpt 1988)), 20-21.

and corruption, hard work by ease-loving, and straightforwardness by deceit and hypocrisy."[329]

The moral degradation also paved the way for changing the value system among the Mizo. The society today is also impacted by the new information technology and globalization with an individualistic attitude. The poor people are suffering due to injustice in the society from the hands of the rich bureaucrats. The elite live in luxurious and consumerist life-style, while the life of the poor people is hard, full of toil and they live a wretched life.[330] In the midst of such a mindset and psychological state of the people the words of comfort and hope preached by Jeremiah is of tremendous significance and value.[331] The church is responsible to give pastoral care and counselling to the people who are under oppression and injustice.

6.3.1.4. Religious Condition

When Christianity has entered into the land of Mizoram, the church faced many obstacles and difficulty. One of the most severe experiences that appeared in the early state of Christianity in Mizoram was persecution.[332] The spread of Christianity was extraordinarily a rapid growth. The fact is, as the number of believers was increasing, the hostility to them was also increasing.[333] Especially the ruling class, i.e. chief class was at daggers with the Mizo converts. So, they were

---

329 Lalmanzuala, "Mizoram at the Crossroads," *Modernization of the Mizo Society*, ed. R. N. Prasad and A. K. Agarwal (New Delhi: A Mittal Publication, 203), 116.

330 Lalrinawma, *Mizo Ethos*, 287-288.

331 Jesurathnam, *Exploring Dalit Liberative Hermeneutics in India & the World*, 311.

332 Saiaithanga, *Mizo Kohhran Chanchin* (Aizawl: The Regional Literature Committee, 1969), 24.

333 C. L. Hminga, *The Life and Witness of the Churches in Mizoram* (Serkawn: The Literature Committee, 1987), 72.

derided and regarded as fools.[334] Some suffered physical torture and were ousted from the village by the chief. Even when they died, Christians were refused for burial.[335] For the Christians at that time life here on earth was full of perils and dangers. Furthermore, Mizo Christians underwent twenty years long military insurgency due to the forces of nationalism. Many people lost their houses, fields, properties and even their lives.[336] All these experiences were so painful and too much depressing to bear. It is no wonder that Mizo Christians who lived in insecure situations were longing for the other world where they would be free from all forms of suffering. The new covenant teaching of comfort and restoration is very much significant for the past, present and future experiences of the church.

6.3.1.5. Condition of the Church

If we look at the condition of the church in Mizoram, the church has responsibility to transform the socio-economic and political life of the people. Joe Laldinpuia observes that in the religious life, we live as if there seems to be no more religious than ours. We construct magnificent church buildings, attend worship services regularly, give tithes regularly, but our inside is full of injustice.[337] With the growing impact of materialism, nominalism, and globalization, the growth of the religious life of the Mizos has slowed down which further affect the socio-ethical life. Religious syncretism is very popular in the Mizo society, where they worship God and materialism together.[338] As a result, many

---

334 Chitta Rajan Nag, *The Mizo Society in Transition* (New Delhi: Vikas Publishing House, 1993), 116.

335 J. M. Lloyd, *On Every High Hill* (Liverpool: Welsh Mission, 1957), 33.

336 On the 1st March 1966, the Mizo National Front declared independence for Mizoram under the leadership of Laldenga, 'Peace Accord' was signed on 30th June, 1986.

337 Joe Laldinpuia, "Amos' Prophetic Response to Injustice Against the Poor in the Israelite Society: A Mizo Tribal Reading," (MTh Thesis, Senate of Serampore, 2015).

338 Lalrinawma, *Mizo Ethos: Changes and Challenges*, 186.

blamed the church for not doing what it supposed to do. In this situation, Jeremiah's message of the new covenant is a paradigm for the church to respond to injustices, discrimination, inequality so that the ethics of equality and egalitarianism can be maintained in the Mizo society and the church.

In Mizoram, the Presbyterian Church in the north and the Baptist Church in the south are the two mainline churches. The administrative divide of south and north Mizoram is also more or less based on the strong geographical divisions of the Presbyterian and the Baptist Church in the state. The other churches made their presence felt in the state much later. Apart from these, many sectarian groups exist with their distinctive beliefs and practices.[339] Previously, there was always a friendly relationship among the denominations. But, as more and more denominations came into existence, however, enticement of members from one church to another and unfriendly relationship among the church leaders of various denominations became very common. A long lasting relationship between the Presbyterian and Baptist Church was disturbed. This conflict has led to the planting of churches in each other's area which resulted in a bitter rivalry between the two churches.[340] In such a situation, forgiveness, one of the ethical teachings of the new covenant, is needed so that all the churches could come together at one table, forgiving one another despite their differences in doctrine or practices.

6.3.2. *Zawlbuk* and *Tlawmngaihna*

As the new covenant taught by Jeremiah served as a guiding principle and acted as a subversive paradigm for the community. For the Mizo Christians, the relationship between ecclesiology and ethics can be looked at and understood in the light of the relation to Mizo Community Home, *Zawlbuk* and Mizo social ethics, *tlawmngaihna*. In other words, it may be said that as the new covenant is the forerunner of the community, for Mizo

339 L. H. Rawsea, "The Eschatological Orientation of Mizo Christianity: Manifestation and Causes," *MTJ*, 6/6 (April-June, 2004), 33.

340 Lalrinawma, *Mizo Ethos: Changes and Challenges*, 186.

community *Zawlbuk* and *tlawmngaihna* are the forerunners of ecclesiology and ethics.[341]

6.3.2.1. *Zawlbuk*

Zawlbuk is a Mizo social institution, which had been established to meet the needs of the community. *Zawlbuk* is described as a community house, dormitory, bachelor house, village house, and community hall. Its literal meaning is flat house.[342] The function of the *Zawlbuk* institution was multiple. The major functions may be described as:[343] (i) Defense of the Village; (ii) Education center; (iii) Recreation Centre; iv) Forum for discussing issues. *Zawlbuk* teaches high ethical principle of *tlawmngaihna* and strict discipline. Thus, the functions of *Zawlbuk* can be effectively appropriated with the new covenant preached Jeremiah. Just as the traditional understanding of *Zawlbuk*, the new covenant was established to meet the needs of the community and taught a highly valued ethical principles for the community. Further, the new covenant can be identified as the church in the NT and the church also teaches ethical life for its members.

6.3.2.2. *Tlawmngaihna*: The Life Giving Principle of the *Zawlbuk*

The most important contribution of the *Zawlbuk* to Mizo society was the development of its giving principle, *tlawmngaihna*. *Tlawmngaihna* is the term used for the Mizo *code of morals*[344]

341 R. Zolawma, "A Critical Assessment of the WCC Study Project "Ecclesiology and Ethics" from a Tribal Perspective," *MTJ*, 8/1 (January-June, 2008): 28.

342 Mangkhosat Kipgen, *Christianity and Mizo Culture* (Jorhat: MTC, 1996), 61-64; Thanzauva, *Theology of Community*, 134-147; N. E. Parry, *A Monograph on Lushai Customs and Ceremonies* (Aizawl: Tribal Research, 1976), 8-10.

343 Zolawma, "A Critical Assessment of the WCC Study Project "Ecclesiology and Ethics" from a Tribal Perspective," *MTJ*: 30.

344 Parry, *A Monograph on Lushai Customs and Ceremonies*, 19.

a *highly prized virtue*[345] and a *wonderful philosophy of life.*[346] A *tlawmngai* person must be obedient and respectful to the elders, courteous in dealing with the weak and the lowly; generous and hospitable to the poor, the needy and the strangers. It may be said that without *tlawmngaihna*, it would not be possible to build a communitarian and a harmonious society where members of the community shared their joy and sorrows and caring one another.[347] The teaching of the new covenant is very much similar to *tlawmngaihna*. Without the new covenant, there cannot be an inclusive and new community envisioned by Jeremiah. As *tlawmngaihna* is marked by obedient, hope, love and care for the poor, the new covenant is also marked by justice and righteousness, forgiveness, solidarity, equality etc.

In the light of the above discussion and comparison, it seems clear that the concept of the new covenant and the Mizo understanding of *Zawlbuk* and *tlawmngaihna* can be effectively appropriated. As the new covenant brings liberation, hope, and new vision towards the community. *Zawlbuk* and *tlawmngaihna* draw the community together and transform the society through its ethical engagement and established a communitarian and harmonious society.

Conclusion

On the basis of the discussions on the new covenant motif and its implications for the community and the church in Mizoram, the following concluding remarks can be observed:

First, from the light of the NT understanding, we find the fulfilment of Jeremiah's new covenant in Jesus Christ. Jesus became the mediator of the new covenant by virtue of his death on the cross. In short, Christians are drawn into the covenant, as

345 J. Meirion Lloyd, *History of the Church in Mizoram* (Aizawl: Synod Publication Board, 1991), 4.

346 N. Chatterji, *Zawlbuk as Social Institution in the Mizo Society* (Aizawl: Tribal Resource Institute, 1975), 15.

347 Zolawma, "A Critical Assessment of the WCC Study Project "Ecclesiology and Ethics" from a Tribal Perspective," *MTJ*: 34.

members of a community of the new covenant. As a result the church has become a new covenant or a new community through the death of Christ on the cross. Moreover, this new covenant is reflected in the coming of God's kingdom in the NT and when such kingdom arrives it will order the entire creation and also ordering of power relationships.[348]

Second, as Jesurathnam has rightly pointed out, the restoration plan and scheme announced by Jeremiah need to be conceived as the holistic vision of God. It is life-enhancing, socially sustainable, enjoyable and richly materials. It also consists of spiritual and psychological reorientation that addresses the questions of personal healing and right governance that would take the course of new creative order.[349]

Third, God's new covenant acts as a subversive paradigm that was initiated with Israelites. It was marked by the ethical framework of justice and righteousness, a new form of Torah, knowledge and forgiveness. It also offers equality, solidarity, egalitarianism and communitarianism. It seeks to emancipate and liberate the community from all forms of oppression and injustice and ensures hope and comfort.

Fourth, the text of the new covenant can be effectively appropriated to the context of the Church in Mizoram. The Church is largely shaped by the socio-economic and political condition. Therefore, the socio-economic and political condition of Mizoram shows that there are many injustices, corruptions, unjust practices in the political sphere as well as in the Church. An enormous gap separated the non-elite from the elite's power, wealth and status. Among the churches and various sectarian groups, there are many conflicts and divisions. Thus, the churches should come together in one voice to create the kingdom of God here on earth.

Fifth, the Mizo traditional social ethics of *Zawlbuk* and *tlawmngaihna* can be effectively related to the ethical framework

348 Jesurathnam, "Socio-Economic and Politico-Religious Horizons of Covenant Community of Israel: Some Ethical Implications," *MJT:* 37-38.

349 Jesurathnam, *Exploring Dalit Liberative Hermeneutics in India & the World*, 310.

of the new covenant. *Zawlbuk* created and maintained co-operation, social solidarity, obedience, loyalty, sense of respect for elders and a sense of mutual help. *Tlawmngaihna* is a social ethic essential for the sustenance of harmony and integrity of the community. It is the backbone that upholds the Mizo-ness of the Mizo;[350] the bone marrow in the cavities of the community that produces the life-giving cells for the poor, destitute, the widows, the downtrodden and the neglected. Therefore, the social ethics of *Zawlbuk* and *tlawmngaihna* must be revived and maintained in order to keep the ethical life and morality of the Church.

Finally, the teaching of the new covenant in Jeremiah remains a powerful tool of liberation and emancipation for any community in the contemporary context where despair and hopeless situation exists. When the communities and individuals experience situations of distress and agony, new covenant in Jeremiah generates a new hope that is promised to all such people.[351]

350 Mizoness of the Mizo is an important factor that upholds their identity. Identity crisis comes when one loses his/her essence or being in the *changing situation.*

351 Jesurathnam, *Exploring Dalit Liberative Hermeneutics in India & the World*, 311.

Chapter 7

General Conclusion

In the light of our preceding observation, it is clear that new covenant motif in Jeremiah does not end in the OT but continues through the NT and it was inaugurated by Jesus Christ who died on the cross. The new covenant has distinctive characters by creating new and inclusive community, justice and righteousness, equality, forgiveness, solidarity and communitarianism, obedience, comfort and hope. The ethical teachings of the new covenant have great implications for the contemporary community and the Church in Mizoram where there are many injustices, corruptions and oppressions. The message of hope and comfort is also very relevant for the poor who suffered under oppression and the church is also responsible to give pastoral care and counselling. From the foregoing study on the new covenant motif in the book of Jeremiah, the following conclusions can be drawn.

1. A study of the socio-historical and political background of Jeremiah is helpful because it provides the wider setting of the context. Jeremiah's context is significant because

he witnessed all the significant events of both the divided kingdoms of ancient Israel and Judah. He also noticed the turmoil and disturbing political situation of the AWA. He was impacted by the overall socio-political, historical and religious developments. Therefore, his thought pattern and theological thinking is influenced by the overall context. He makes use of the combination of covenantal motifs, divine pathos to critique and subvert the extraordinary claims of royal-temple ideology. He talks about the triumph as well as disaster in unequivocal terms for the welfare of the community of Judah. He was not in search of some political answers for the crises situation, rather return to the basic covenant stipulations that the community had lost in their faith journey.

2. An analysis of covenant in the ancient and biblical world reveals that it was from the period of Deuteronomy and Jeremiah onwards that *bĕrît* became a term emphasized and central importance in Israelite religion. Regarding the meaning and definition of the word, there was no consensus among scholars. The etymological study shows that the concept of covenant is not determined by the term *bĕrît* itself rather it is determined by the basis of the relationship with God. The study also reveals that there are convergences as well as divergences between the OT covenant and AWA treaties. Further, the concept of covenant has been developed and changed from time to time according to the context and their needs. Therefore, there was a shift from the exclusive nature of the covenant to inclusivity.
3. The exegetical study of the covenant texts shows that Jeremiah used several covenant traditions and formulas. There is a significant shift and change in the use and function of the covenant formula. First, the formula is related to the deliverance from Egypt and the demands that God had made with the Israelite that the people should listen to God's voice. Second, the prophet wants to affirm the demands of the Sinai covenant as against the people who cherish royal covenant upheld by the leaders in Jerusalem. Third, *the covenant*

formula points to the future. It is announced for the salvific future still impending in which Israel will then turn back to God with its whole and new heart. God will make a new beginning, which will be subject to the covenant formula, as the summary expression of God's relationship to God's people. Fourth, the formula points to the promise of single heart and single nature. It was very similar to the promise in the new covenant. The everlasting covenant is to take effect on the exilic community after its return to the land.

4. The old covenant has its own limitations due to the changing circumstances and situations. Therefore, Jeremiah shifted his thinking of the old covenant to the new covenant that God has promised a new covenant, not like the previous covenant which is based on justice and righteousness. There will be common, shared access to the knowledge which evidences fundamental egalitarianism in the community. God will forgive their iniquities and remember their sins no more. Thus, the text of the new covenant can be effectively appropriated to the context of the Church in Mizoram.
5. From the light of the NT understanding, we find the fulfilment of Jeremiah's new covenant in Jesus Christ. In short, Christians are drawn into the covenant, as members of a community of the new covenant. As a result the Church has become a new covenant or a new community. The socio-economic, political and religious condition of Mizoram reveals that there are many injustices, corruptions, discrimination and inequality. The study proposes the Mizo traditional social ethics of *Zawlbuk* and *tlawmngaihna* as an ethical framework of the new covenant. God's new covenant acts as a subversive paradigm and offers equality, solidarity, egalitarianism and communitarianism. It seeks to emancipate and liberate the community from all forms of oppression and injustice and ensures hope and comfort.

Bibliography

1. Primary Sources

Brown, Francis, S. R. Driver and Charles A. Briggs. *A Hebrew and English Lexicon of the Old Testament.* Oxford: Clarendon Press, 1979.

Ellinger, K. and W. Rudolph. *Biblia Hebraica Stuttgartensia.* Stuttgart: Deutsch Bibelgesellschaft, 1997.

The Holy Bible. *The New Revised Standard Version.* Catholic Edition for India. Bangalore: Theological Publications in India, 1996.

2. Secondary Sources

2.1. Monographs

Adeyemi, F. *The New Covenant Torah in Jeremiah and the Law of Christ in Paul*. New York: Peter Lang, 2006.

Allis, Oswald T. *Prophecy and the Church.* Philadelphia: Presbyterian and Reformed, 1945.

Baltzer, Klaus. *The Covenant Formulary: In Old Testament, Jewish, and Early Christian Writings*. Trans. David E. Green. Oxford: Basil Blackwell, 1971.

Barr, James. *The Semantic Biblical Language*. Glasgow: Oxford University Press, 1961.

Bozak, B. *Life 'Anew:' A Literary-Theological Study of Jer. 30-31*. Analecta Biblica 122. Roma: Gregorian Biblical Book Shop, 1991.

Bright, John. "The Date of the Prose Sermons of Jeremiah." *A Prophet to the Nations: Essays in Jeremiah Studies*. Eds. Leo G. Perdue and Brian W. Kovacs. Winona Lake, Indiana: Eisenbraunts, 1984, 193-212.

_______. *A History of Israel.* Third Edition. London: SCM Press Ltd, 1964.

Brueggemann, Walter. *A Social Reading of the Old Testament: Prophetic Approaches of Israel's Communal Life*. Ed. Patrick D. Miller. Minneapolis: Fortress Press, 1994.

_______. "The Book of Jeremiah: Portrait of the Prophet." *Interpreting the Prophets*. Eds. James L. Mays and Paul J. Achtemeier. Philadelphia: Fortress Press, 1987, 113-129.

Bultmann, R. *Theology of the New Testament.* 2 Vols. Trans. K. Grobel. Texas: Baylor University Press, 2007.

Buss, Martin J. Review of *Bundestheologies im Alten Testament*, by Lothar Perlitt. *JBL* 90/2 (1971): 210-212.

Calvin, John. *Institutes of the Christian Religion*. Trans. Ford Lewis Battles. Philadelphia: Westminster, 1971.

Carroll, Robert P. *From Chaos to Covenant: Prophecy in the Book of Jeremiah*. New York: SCM, 1981.

Ceresko, Anthony R. *The Old Testament: A Liberation Perspective*. Bangalore: St. Paul, 1993.

Chatterjee, Suhas. *Mizoram Under the British Rule*. New Delhi: Mittal Publications, 1985.

Chatterji, N. *Zawlbuk as Social Institution in the Mizo Society*. Aizawl: Tribal Resource Institute, 1975.

Clements, R. E. *A Century of Old Testament Study*. London: Lutterworth Press, 1976.

_______. *Prophecy and Covenant*. London: SCM Press, 1965.

_______. *Jeremiah, Interpretation*. Atlanta: John Knox, 1988

Collins, T. *The Mantle of Elijah: The Redaction Criticism of the Prophetical Books*. Sheffield: JSOT Press, 1993.

Dumbell, William J. *Covenant and Creation: An Old Testament Covenant Theology*. Lancer: The Paternoster Press, 1984.

Dyrness, William. *Themes of the Old Testament Theology*. Illinois: Intervarsity Press, 1979.

Eichrodt, Walther. *Theology of the Old Testament*. Vol. I. Trans. J. A. Baker. London: SCM Press Ltd.1961.

Gottwald, Norman K. *The Hebrew Bible: A Socio-Literary Introduction*. Philadelphia: Fortress Press, 1987.

Harrison, R. K. *Introduction to the Old Testament*. Grand Rapids: Eerdmans, 1969.

Hasel, Gerhard. *Old Testament Theology: Basic Issues in the Current Debates*. Revised Edition. Grand Rapids: William B. Eerdmans Publishing Co., 1979.

Hillers, Delbert R. *Covenant: The History of a Biblical Idea*. Baltimore: John Hopkins University Press, 1969.

Hminga, C. L. *The Life and Witness of the Churches in Mizoram*. Serkawn: The Literature Committee, 1987.

Holladay, W. L. *Jeremiah: Spokesman Out of Time*. Philadelphia: United Church Press, 1974.

Hyatt, J. Philip. "The Deuteronomic Edition of Jeremiah." *A Prophet to the Nations: Essays in Jeremiah Studies*. Eds. Leo G. Perdue and Brian W. Kovacs. Winona Lake, Indiana: Eisenbraunts, 1984, 247-267.

Jacob, Edmond. *Theology of the Old Testament*. Trans. Arthur W. Heathcote and Philip J. Allcock. New York: Harper and Brothers, 1958.

Jesurathnam, K. "Transforming Praxis: God, Community, Church-Reading Jeremiah 7:1-15 (Temple Sermon with Special Focus on Dalit Christian Response)." *Transforming Praxis: God, Community and Church, Essays in Honour of Dr. I. John Mohan Razu*. Ed. C. I. David Joy. Bangalore: UTC, 2008, 111-132.

_______. *Old Testament Theology: History, Issues, and Perspectives*. New Delhi: Christian World Imprints, 2016.

Joüon P. & T. Muraoka. *A Grammar of Biblical Hebrew,* 2nd ed. Subsidia Biblica, 27. Rome: Editrice Pontificio Istituto Biblico, 2006.

Kaiser Jr., Walter C. "The Law as God's Gracious Guidance for the Promotion of Holiness." *Five Views on Law and Gospel*. Ed. Wayne G. Strickland. Grand Rapids: Zondervan, 1996, 189-304.

_______. *Toward an Old Testament Theology*. Grand Rapids: Zondervan, 1978.

_______. *Toward Rediscovering the Old Testament*. Grand Rapids: Zondervan, 1987.

Kalluveettil, Paul. *Declaration and Covenant: A Comprehensive Review of Covenant Formulae from the Old Testament and the Ancient Near East*. Rome: Biblical Institute Press, 1982.

Kearney, Peter J. Review of *Bundestheologies im Alten Testament*, by Lothar Perlitt. *CBQ* 34 (1972): 524-528.

Kipgen, Mangkhosat. *Christianity and Mizo Culture*. Jorhat: MTC, 1996.

Kizhakkeyil, Sebastian. *Jeremiah: An Exegetical Commentary*. Bangalore: ATC, 2006.

Lallawmzuala, K. "Sem Sem Dam Dam, Ei Bil Thi Thi." *Hmatiang Sawnin* (Move Forward). Bangalore: Shalom Publication, 2001, 260-285.

Lallungmuana, H. "Mizo Culture and Christianity." *Kum Za Mel Lung*. Eds. Vanlalnghaka Ralte, et al. Aizawl: Aizawl Theological College, 2007, 172-176.

Lalmanzuala. "Mizoram at the Crossroads." *Modernization of the Mizo Society*. Eds. R. N. Prasad and A. K. Agarwal, New Delhi: A Mittal Publication, 203, 95-129.

Lalnithanga, P. *Emergence of Mizoram*. 2nd Edition. Aizawl: P. Lalnithanga, 2005.

Lalrinawma, V. S. *Mizo Ethos: Changes and Challenges*. Aizawl: Mizoram Publication Board, 2005.

Lalrinthanga, H. *Church and State: Relationship in the Mizo Socio-Political Life 1952 to 2006*. Delhi: ISPCK, 2013.

Leena, Henk. *Newness in Old Testament Prophecy: An Intertextual Study*. Leiden-Boston: Brill, 2014.

Lemche, Niels Peter. *Ancient Israel: A New History of Israelite Society*. Sheffield: JSOT Press, 1990.

Lloyd, J. Meirion. *History of the Church in Mizoram*. Aizawl: Synod Publication Board, 1991.

Lloyd, J. M. *On Every High Hill*. Liverpool: Welsh Mission, 1957.

Longchar, A. Wati. "The Need for Studying Tribal Theology." *An Exploration of Tribal Theology*. Edited by A. Wati Longchar. Jorhat: The Tribal Study Centre, 1997, 1-20.

Malsawma, H. L. *Sociology of the Mizos*. Guwahati: Spectrum Publications, 2002.

Mathew, P. C. *Berith: The Semitic Concept of Divine Human Relationship*. Kottayam: Ashram Press, 1987.

McCarthy, Dennis J. Review of *Bundestheologies im Alten Testament*, by Lothar Perlitt. *Biblica* 53/1 (1972): 110-121.

_______. *Treaty and Covenant: A Study in Form in the Ancient Oriental Documents and in the Old Testament*. Rome: Pontifical Biblical Institute, 1963.

Muraoka, T. *Emphatic Words and Structures in Biblical Hebrew*. Jerusalem: Magnes Press, 1985.

Muthunayagom, Daniel Jones. "Contemporary Approaches to Old Testament Interpretation." *Interweaving Methodology and Praxis: Exploring Disciplinary Options in Today's World.* Edited by Indukuri John Mohan Raju. Bangalore: BTESSC, 2007, 169-204.

Nag, Chitta Rajan. *Mizo Polity and Political Modernization.* Delhi: Vikash Publishing House Pvt. Ltd., 1988.

_______. *The Mizo Society in Transition.* New Delhi: Vikas Publishing House, 1993.

Newman, Barclay M. and Philip C. Stine. *A Handbook on Jeremiah.* New York : United Bible Societies, 2003.

Nicholson, E. W. *Preaching to the Exiles: A Study of the Prose Tradition in the Book of Jeremiah.* Basil: Blackwell, 1970.

_______. *God and His People: Covenant and Theology in the Old Testament.* Oxford: Clarendon Press, 1986.

Noth, Martin. *The Laws in the Pentateuch and Other Studies.* Trans. D. R. Ap-Thomas. Edinburgh and London: Oliver & Boyd, 1967.

Oded, Bustenay. "Judah and the Exile." *Israelite and Judaean History.* Eds. John H. Hayes and J. Maxwell Miller. London: SCM Press Ltd., 1977, 435-486.

Parry, N. E. *A Monograph on Lushai Customs and Ceremonies.* Aizawl: Tribal Research, 1976.

Pedersen, Johs. *Israel: Its life and Culture.* Vols. I-II. London: Oxford University Press, 1959.

Pitchard, James B. *Ancient Near Eastern Texts.* Princeton: Princeton University Press, 1950.

Rata, Tiberius. *The Covenant Motif in Jeremiah's Book of Comfort: Textual and Intertextual Studies of Jeremiah 30-33.* New York: Peter Lang, 2007.

Rendtorff, Rolf. *The Covenant Formula: An Exegetical and Theological Investigation.* Edinburg: T&T Clark, 1998.

Roberts, J. J. "Ancient Near Eastern Environment." *The Hebrew Bible and Its Modern Interpreters.* Ed. Knight and Tucker. Philadelphia: Fortress Press, 1985, 75-96.

Rudolph, W. *Jeremia*. Tübingen: Mohr (Siebeck), 1968.

Saiaithanga. *Mizo Kohhran Chanchin*. Aizawl: The Regional Literature Committee, 1969.

Shakespeare, J. *The Lushai Kuki Clans*. Aizawl: Tribal Research Institute, 1912 (rpt. 1988).

Sangkima. *Essays on the History of the Mizos*. Guwahati: Spectrum Publications, 2004.

Sarason, R. S. "The Interpretation of Jeremiah 31:31-34 in Judaism." *When Jesus and Christians Meet*. Ed. Petuchowski. J. J. Albany: State University of New York Press, 1988, 99-112.

Seilhamer, Frank H. *The New Covenant in Jeremiah 31:31-34 and Its Place in the Covenant-Treaty Tradition of Israel and the Ancient Near East*. Springfield, OH: New World, 1976.

Showers, Renald E. *There Really Is a Difference: A Comparison of Covenant and Dispensational Theology*. Bellmawr, NJ: Friends of Israel, 1990.

Siegfried, Herrmann. *A History of Israel in Old Testament Times*. London: SCM Press Ltd, 1975.

Smith, Ralph L. *Old Testament Theology: Its History, Method, and Message*. Nashville: Broadman & Holman Publishers, 1993.

Thanzauva, K. *Theology of Community*. Bangalore: Asian Trading Corporation, 2004.

Thompson, J. A. *The Ancient Near Eastern Treaties and the Old Testament*. London: Tyndale, 1964.

Tov, E. *Textual Criticism of the Hebrew Bible*. 2nd Rev. Ed. Minneapolis: Fortress Press, 1992.

Unterman, Jeremiah. *From Repentance to Redemption: Jeremiah's Thought in Transition*. JSOT Sup54. Sheffield: Sheffield Academic, 1987.

Vanlalchhuanawma & Rosiamliana Tochhawng. "Identification of Communalities and Divergence in Doing Theology from Tribal Perspective." *Dalit-Tribal Theological Interface: Current Trends in Subaltern Theologies*. Eds. James Massey and Shimreingam Shimray. TSC/WSC: ETC Jorhat, 2007, 218-245.

Vallianippuram, Thomas. *Jeremiah: A Prophet of the Modern World.* Bangalore: Dharmaram Publications, 2012.

Verghese, C. G. and R. L. Thanzawna. *A History of the Mizos.* Vol. 1. New Delhi: Vikas Publishing House Pvt. Ltd., 1997.

von Rad, Gerhard. *Old Testament Theology: The Theology of Israel's Prophetic Traditions.* Vol. 2. Trans. D. M. G. Stalker. Edinburgh & London: Oliver & Boyd, 1965.

_______. *The Problem of Hexateuch and Other Essays.* Edinburgh: Oliver & Boyd, 1966.

Vries, S. J. de. *From Old Revelation to New: A Tradition-Historical and Redaction-Critical Study of Temporal Transitions in Prophetic Prediction.* Grand Rapids: Eerdmans, 1995.

Wienfeld, M. *Deuteronomy and Deuteronomic School.* Oxford: Clarendon Press, 1972.

Wolff, H. W. *Confrontations with Prophets.* Philadelphia: Fortress, 1983.

Zimmerli, Walther. "Visionary Experience in Jeremiah." *Israel's Prophetic Tradition: Essays in Honour of Peter R. Ackroyd.* Eds. R. Coggins et al. Cambridge: University Press, 1982, 95-118.

_______. "The History of Israelite Religion." *Tradition and Interpretation.* Ed. G. W. Anderson. Philadelphia: Fortress Press, 1979, 379-380.

_______. *Old Testament Theology in Outline.* Atlanta: John Knox Press, 1978.

2.2. Commentaries

Blackwood, A.W. *Commentary on Jeremiah.* Waco: Word, 1977.

Bracke, John M. *Jeremiah 1-29, Westminster Bible Companion.* Westminster: John Knox Press, 2000.

_______. *Jeremiah 30-52 and Lamentations, Westminster Bible Companion*. Louisveill, Kentucky: Westinster John Knox Press, 2000.

Bright, John. *Jeremiah: A New Translation with Introduction and Commentary*: *AB*. New York: Double Day Company, 1965.

Brueggemann, Walter. *A Commentary on Jeremiah: Exile and Homecoming*. Grand Rapids/Cambridge: William B. Eerdmans Publishing Company, 1998.

_______. *To Build, To Plant: A Commentary on Jeremiah 26–52*. Grand Rapids: Eerdmans, 1991.

Calvin, John. *Commentaries on the Book of the Prophet Jeremiah and Lamentations*. Vol. 4. Trans. John Owen. Edinburgh: Calvin Translation Society, 1850; reprint, Grand Rapids: Eerdmans, 1950.

Carroll, Robert P. *Jeremiah: A Commentary*. Philadelphia: Westminster Press, 1986.

Craigie, Peter C. *Jeremiah 1-25: WBC*. Vol. 26. Dallas : Word, Incorporated, 2002.

Holladay, William L. *Jeremiah 1: A Commentary on the Book of Prophet Jeremiah Chapters 1-25*. Philadelphia: Fortress Press, 1986.

Holladay, William L. *Jeremiah 2: A Commentary on the Book of the Prophet Jeremiah Chapters 26-52*. Philadelphia: Fortress Press, 1990.

Huey, F. B. *Jeremiah, Lamentations: NAC*. Vol. 16. Nashville: Broadman & Holman Publishers, 1993.

Hyatt, J. P. "The Book of Jeremiah." *IB*. 12 Vols. Edited by G. A. Buttrick et al. (Nashville: Abingdon Press, 1956), 777-1142.

Jesurathnam, Kondasingu. *Exploring Dalit Liberative Hermeneutics in India & The World: Based on an Ancient Hebrew Prophet, Jeremiah of Anathoth*. New Delhi: Christian World Imprints, 2015.

Keown, Gerald L. *Jeremiah 26-52: WBC*. Vol. 27. Dallas : Word, Incorporated, 2002.

Lundbom, J. R. *Jeremiah 1-20*: *AB*. New York: Doubleday, 1999.

McKane, W. *A Critical and Exegetical Commentary on Jeremiah*. Edinburg: T&T Clark, 1986.

Miller, Patrick D. "The Book of Jeremiah: Introduction, Commentary, and Reflections." *NIB*. Vol. IV (Nashville: Abingdon Press, 2001): 553-926.

Nicholson, E. W. *Jeremiah 1-25: Cambridge Bible Commentary on the New English Bible*. Cambridge University Press: Cambridge, 1973.

Thompson, J. A. *The Book of Jeremiah: NICOT*. Grand Rapids, Michigan: William B. Eerdmans Publishing Company, 1980.

2.3. Encyclopaedias, Dictionaries and Lexicons

Beaulieu, P. A. "History of Israel 6: Babylonian Period." *Dictionary of the Old Testament: Historical Books*. Eds. Bill T. Arnold and H. G. M. Williamson. Illinois: InterVarsity Press, 2005, 478-485.

Behm, Johannes. "Kaino." *TDNT*. Vol. III. Ed. Gerhard Kittel. Trans. Geoffrey W. Bromiley. Grand Rapids: Eerdmans, 1965, 447-450.

Campbell, W. S. "Covenant and New Covenant." *Dictionary of Paul and His Letters*. Eds. Gerald F. Hawthorne, Ralph P. Martin & Daniel G. Reid. Downers Grove, Illinois: InterVarsity Press, 1993, 179-182.

Elwell, Walter A. & Philip Wesley Comfort. *Tyndale Bible Dictionary*. Wheaton, Illinois: Tyndale House Publishers, 2001.

Goldingay, John. "Covenant, OT and NT." *NIDB*. Vol. 1. Eds. K. D. Sekenfeld et al. Nashville: Abingdon Press, 2006, 767-778.

Harris, R. L. G. L. Archer, & B. K. Waltke. *Theological Wordbook of the Old Testament*. Chicago: Moody Press, 1980.

Koehler, Ludwig and Walter Baumgartner. *The Hebrew and Aramaic Lexicon of the Old Testament*. Vol. I. Trans. and Ed. M. E. J. Richardson. New York: E. J. Brill, 1994.

Kutch, E. "בְּרִית." *Theological Lexicon of the Old Testament.* Vol. I. Eds. Ernst Jenni and Claus Westermann (Peabody: Hendrickson Publishers, Inc., 1997), 256-266.

Lundbom, Jack R. "Jeremiah (Prophet)." *ABD*. Vol. 3. Eds. David Noel Freedman, et al. New York: Doubleday, 1992, 684-698.

Lundbom, Jack R. "New Covenant." *ABD*. Vol. 4. Eds. David Noel Freedman, et al. London: Doubleday, 1992, 1088-1094.

Mendenhall, George E. "Covenant." *IDB*. Vol. I. Eds. George Arthur Buttrick, et al. Nashville: Abingdon Press, 1962, 714-723.

Mendenhall, George E. and Gary A. Herion. "Covenant." *ABD*. Vol. I. Eds. David Noel Freedman, et al. London: Doubleday, 1992, 1179-1202.

Perlitt, Lothar. "Covenant." *The Encyclopedia of Christianity*. Vol. 1. Eds. Erwin Fahlbusch et al (Grand Rapids, Michigan: William B. Eerdmans Publishing Company, 1997), 709-711.

Rata, T. "Covenant." *Dictionary of Old Testament: Prophets*. Eds. Mark J. Boda & J. Gordon McConville. Downers Grove: InterVarsity Press, 2012, 99-104.

Verhoef, Pieter A. "חָדָשׁ." *NIDOTTE*. Ed. Willem A. VanGemeren. Grand Rapids: Zondervan, 1997, 30-37.

Weinfeld, M. "בְּרִית." *TDOT.* Vol. II. Eds. G. Johannes, Botterweck and Helmer Ringgren. Trans. John T. Willis. Grand Rapids: William B. Eerdmans Publishing Company, 1977, 254-255.

Williamson, P. R. "Covenant." *Dictionary of the Old Testament Pentateuch*. Eds. T. Desmond Alexander and David W. Baker. Secunderabad: OM Authentic Books, 2007, 139-155.

2.4. Journals/Periodicals

Baker, J. Coleman. "New Covenant, New Identity: A Social-Scientific Reading of Jeremiah 31:31-34." *The Bible and Critical Theory* 4/1 (2008): 5.1-5.11.

Becking, Bob "Text-Internal and Text-External Chronology in Jeremiah 31:31-34," *SEA* 61 (1996): 32-50.

Biddle, M. "The Literary Frame Surrounding Jeremiah 30:1-33:26." *ZAW* 100 (1988): 409-413.

Bright, John. "An Exercise in Hermeneutics Jeremiah 31 31-34." *Interpretation* 20 (1966): 188-210.

Brueggemann, Walter. "The Book of Jeremiah: Portrait of the Prophet." *Interpretation* 37 (1983): 130-145.

Gerstenberger, Erhard. "Covenant and Commandment." *VT* 84/1 (March 1965): 38-51.

Jathana, C. D. "The Covenant and Covenant Making in Pentateuch." *BTF* 3/1, (Jan-June, 1969): 27-54.

Jesurathnam, K. "'Before I Formed You in the Womb of Your Mother:' The Decentred World of Jeremiah and Dalits." *BTF* XLIII/1 (June 2011): 1-40.

_______. "Socio-Economic and Politico-Religious Horizons of Covenant Community of Israel: Some Ethical Implications." *MJT* 4/2 (December, 2014): 24-46.

Kaiser, Walter C. "The Old Promise and the New Covenant: Jeremiah 31:31-34." *JETS* 15 (1972): 11-23.

Koehler, Ludwig. "Problems in the Study of the Language of the Old Testament." *JSS* 1/1, (January, 1956): 3-24.

Lemke, Werner E. "Jeremiah 31:31-34." *Interpretation* 37 (1983): 183-187.

McCarthy, Dennis J. "Covenant in the Old Testament: The Present State of Inquiry." *CBQ* 27 (1965): 217-240.

McConville, J. G. "Jeremiah: Prophet and Book," *Tyndale Bulletin* 42 (1991): 93.

Miller Jr., Patrick D. "The Gift of God: The Deuteronomic Theology of the Land." *Interpretation* 23 (1969): 451-465.

Moulton, W. J. "The New Covenant in Jeremiah." *The Expositor*, Series 7,1 (1906): 370-382.

Muilenburg, J. "The form and Structure of the Covenant Formulations." *VT* 9 (1959): 347-365.

Overholt, T. W. "Some Reflections on the Date of Jeremiah's Call." *CBQ* 33 (1971): 165-184.

Pachuau, Lalsangkima. "Tribal" Identity and Ethnic Conflicts in Northeast India: A "Tribal" Christian Response." *BTF* XXXI/1 (July, 1999): 157-167.

Potter, H.D. "The New Covenant in Jeremiah XXXI 31-34." *VT* 33/3(July 1983): 347-355.

Rawsea, L. H. "The Eschatological Orientation of Mizo Christianity: Manifestation and Causes." *MTJ* 6/6 (April-June, 2004): 18-38.

Rom-Shiloni, Dalit. "The Prophecy for "Everlasting Covenant" (Jeremiah XXXII 36-41): An Exilic Addition or A Deuteronomistic Redactions?" *VT* LIII/2 (2003): 201-223.

Sangliana, H. T. "Why Corruption in Christian State Mizoram?" *Chhinlung* 14 (2002-2003): 58-81.

Swetnam, J. "Why was Jeremiah's New Covenant New?" *SVT* 26 (1974): 111-15.

Talbert, Charles H. "Paul on the Covenant." *Review and Expositor* 84 (1987): 299-300.

Vallianippuram, Thomas. "*Mispat* and *Sedaqa*: The Vision of Social Justice in Jeremiah." *Bible Bhashyam* 34/4 (2010): 321-355.

Vanlalauva, H. "Role of the Churches in Mizoram." *MTJ* 6/1 (January-June, 2006): 5-18.

Wang, Martin Cheng-Chang. "Jeremiah and the Covenant Tradition." *SEAJT* 14/1 (1972): 3-13.

Weinfeld, M. "Jeremiah and the Spiritual Metamorphosis of Israel." *ZAW* 88 (1976): 17-56.

Weinfeld, M. "The Covenant of Grant in the Old Testament and in the Ancient Near East." *Journal of the American Oriental Society* 90 (1970): 185.

Zolawma, R. "A Critical Assessment of the WCC Study Project "Ecclesiology and Ethics" from a Tribal Perspective." *MTJ*, 8/1 (January-June, 2008): 14-44.

2.5. Unpublished Thesis/Dissertation

Jathana, C. D. "*The Covenant and Covenant Making in Pentateuch*." DTh Dissertation, Hamburg University, 1967.

Laldinpuia, Joe. "*Amos' Prophetic Response to Injustice Against the Poor in the Israelite Society: A Mizo Tribal Reading*." MTh Thesis, Senate of Serampore, 2015.